The Chronicles
Zen Ramblings from the Internet

Scott Shaw

Buddha Rose Publications

The Chronicles:
Zen Ramblings from the Internet
Copyright © 2013 by Scott Shaw
All Rights Reserved
www.scottshaw.com

Rear cover photograph of Scott Shaw
by Hae Won Shin
Copyright © 2013 All Rights Reserved

First Edition 2013

ISBN: 1-877792-73-X
ISBN 13: 978-1-877792-73-1
Library of Congress: 2013951711

No part of this book may be reproduced in any manner without the expressed written permission of the author or the publishing company.

Printed in the United States of America

10 9 8 7 6 5 4 3 2 1

The Chronicles
Zen Ramblings from the Internet

...*Contents*

Introduction	**11**
There's a Lot of Violence Going On...	**14**
Speculation	**16**
Personal Impact	**18**
What Do You Mean By That?	**20**
Things Aren't Always What They Seem.	**22**
You're Either Doing Something Positive or You're Doing Something Negative. But, which is which?	**24**
My Air Conditioner is Broken!	**26**
On Your Own	**27**
When I Was Young...	**29**
Listen To How You Walk	**32**
Life: Love or Hate	**33**
Soma	**34**
The Impact That You're Having	**36**
Momentary Reality	**38**
Nobody Wants to Die	**41**
Where is Knowledge Based?	**43**
Wild in the Streets	**46**
Know Who You Are	**48**
Conflict	**50**
What People Believe	**52**

I'm Glad You Know So Much More Than Me. Maybe You Should Be the One Writing the Books.	**54**
The Road You're On	**56**
Thinking	**58**
Stand Up For Your Rights	**59**
The Quality of Sound	**62**
You Will Not Remember This Moment	**64**
Knowing What You Don't Know	**66**
Alone or Together	**69**
My Way or the Highway	**72**
You Talk Too Loud	**74**
Liar	**77**
Fading Out	**79**
Sometimes You See Strange Things	**81**
Scott Shaw Likes	**82**
Freedom in the Hail	**84**
Don't Let Your Eggs Get Cold	**86**
The Powers That Be	**88**
I Don't Want to Do Anything	**91**
People Don't Want to Know the Truth	**93**
Snitch	**94**
Dysfunctional Insanity	**98**
The Beachside Table	**100**
Art is Everywhere	**102**
The End of Days	**103**

Painting on Paper	**106**
Answers Verses Opinions	**108**
2nd	**110**
Everything Used To Be On Wheels	**112**
Remember When It Was So Important To Watch Music Videos?	**113**
Nobody Wants to See Old People Dance	**115**
Where You Plant Your Seeds	**117**
Belief	**119**
Somebody Told Me	**121**
The Lab	**123**
Do You Think About Others Before You Do What You Do?	**125**
People Fall Away	**127**
Process Verse Product	**130**
Your Past Haunts You	**132**
Creation and Adaptation	**134**
Charity or Not?	**138**
Yes Madam. Yes Sir.	**140**
The Earth Still Spins	**142**
Don't Do Things That Hurt People	**144**
Everything Has Already Been Done	**146**
Walk Around the Block	**148**
Everything is Made in China	**149**
Art or Obsession?	**152**
Youth Is An Interesting Place	**154**

Have You Hurt Somebody?	**157**
Desire Verse Drive	**159**
Chinatown Bong	**161**
Martial Arts on the Spiritual Path	**164**
That's Life/That's Work	**168**
Is Painting an Accomplishment?	**170**
You Weren't There So You Don't Know	**172**
Tell Them Willy Boy Is Here	**174**
Thank You For Your Kindness	**177**
Everybody Wants a Better Life	**179**
Friend or Foe	**181**
Too Famous. …For All the Wrong Reasons.	**184**
Seeing Who You Don't Want To See	**188**
Something is Lost in the Recording	**191**
Claiming Spirituality	**193**
Monkey Wrench in the Gears	**195**
Inside the Corner	**197**
Any Less Enlightened?	**199**
Sometime You Just Have To Buy a New Pair of Shoes	**201**
When Opportunity Comes Knocking	**205**
Texting on Two Wheels	**207**
A Choice Lasts Forever	**209**
In or Out	**211**
You Verses Who	**214**

Sometime You Get Cut	**216**
About the Author	**219**
Scott Shaw *Books-in-Print*	**220**

...Introduction: Zen Blog 2.0

Due to ongoing requests, I am going to try to get back into blogging. But, I feel like I must say a few things at the outset…

For those of you who know, (or don't know), I used to blog but then it just started to get really-really weird. People would show up at the places I mentioned in the blog and pretended that they were so surprised to run into me. Or, I would notice someone sitting across the courtyard, staring at me, if I was having a *latte'* or something. Some people would even show up and hang out at my P.O. Box to see me going to get my mail and then they would try to follow me home or to where ever it was that I was driving. Weird, weird, weird !!!

People, you don't have to stalk me! I live a fairly uneventful life. So, this kind of nonsense is really unnecessary. And, I am the most approachable person in the world. If you want to communicate with me, simply contact me. As long as you are cool, so am I…

The other side of the weirdness came via the Internet. Some people would email me really rude comments just to see if I would respond or mention them in my blog. Or, they would write something really negative or untrue about me on some website, (out there in cyberspace), and then email me the location. Again, just to see if they could get a rise out of me so that I would mention them in the blog. But, believe me, I really don't care what some anonymous person, who hides behind a screen name, has to say about me or anyone else.

You know, I understand that there are a lot of adolescences and adolescent minded people out there, who really don't have anything better to do than to patrol the Internet looking for someone or something to love or to hate. But, that is their fault. There is a lot of life to live. Get off the Internet and live it! And, as I always say, you should really get out there and create something positive in your chosen field of art. Then, you don't have to waste your Life-Time thinking about, discussing, and critiquing the work of others.

    This being stated, at the outset of this new blog I believe it is really important to note, if you are going to misquote me or use my words out of context as a means to get your own name out there while you formulate some misguided point about my projects or myself, all that does is make you look like your own words are not worthy or that you do not have anything of your own worth stating. So, don't waste your time! It's not going to change me or my world in any way, shape, or form. And, I'm not going to mention you in the blog. Ultimately, it just makes YOU look bad. So instead, get out there, LIVE and CREATE your own life and your own art!

    And then... OMG, there were the people who just knew I was writing whatever I was writing about them. This, when I didn't even know who they were or, if I did know them, I wasn't even thinking about 'em. They would contact me and tell me what they thought about me writing about them. Awh, the paranoid... It wasn't about you !!! If it was, I would tell you.

    I have always found that in life most people are really cool. Others, for whatever reason, are not. They are motivated by greed, desire, ego, superiority, insecurity, whatever... This being stated, I really only want to associate and communicate with nice people who don't have some weird, self-serving agenda. And, that will be the basis of this new blog. Keep any negativity to yourself!

For the, *what-ever-it-is-worth,* my previous blog was published as a book entitled, *Scribbles on the Restroom Wall.* The introduction to that book goes into much more detail about some of the occurrences that took place and some of my motivations for writing and then discontinuing the original blog. It also has all of the blog entries that I wrote. So, if you're interested, feel free to check it out.

Also, I guess I should mention that I do my blogging stream-of-consciousness style, so you may see some typos. I toss that to the world of, whatever... As long as the ideas get out there...

Okay, that's the basis. Hopefully we can have some fun with this blog again. I can write about what I am thinking and what I am doing... For those of you who liked to read the original blog, you will have something new to read. But, if it gets weird again, then I guess I will just have to cease writing. Hopefully that won't happen.

But for now, *Let the Blogging Recommence!*

That was then... This is now...

I blogged for awhile, then the previously described nonsense all began all over again. So, I found it necessary to turn off the blog AGAIN. But, for those of you who enjoyed it, (or did not yet have the chance to read it), here it is, in its entirety. *The Scott Shaw Zen Blog 2.0.*

There's a Lot of Violence Going On

There's a lot of violence going on...

Not to mention the meaningless violence that took place at the Batman movie two weeks ago, yesterday there was a shooting at a Sikh temple. It turns out it was apparently done by an army veteran.

Have you ever had violence unleashed against you? If you have, you know it is not very nice.

Have you ever unleashed violence against someone one else? If you have, though you may have gained a sense of momentary power and an adrenaline rush, that fades and all that is left is a new set of life-problems you will need to overcome.

Violence takes place in all kinds of ways and on all kinds of levels. Where I grew up, (on the wrong side of the tracks in L.A.), I constantly saw violence. And, it was always performed by someone who held the advantage. Either a gang of people who accosted one person or someone with a knife or a gun who would go after an individual. They did this because they obviously held the advantage due to their numbers or their weapon.

Even in India, where the Sikh religion was born, there is a lot of violence. ...Based on the fact of too many people in too small of a space, I guess?

Though many people assume that India is a universally holy place, this is not, necessarily, the case.

I remember the first time I traveled to India, I was riding around in one of those three wheeled taxis in Delhi and the driver apparently did something wrong. A traffic cop came up and began literally smacking the guy in the head.

When I was in places like the holy city of Varanasi, some people would throw rocks at me, (behind my back, when I wasn't looking, of course), I guess just because I was white.

Later, when I took sannyas, and wore an orange robe, people would run up and touch my feet, seeking my blessings. India, a complex society... Extreme violence and extreme holiness. And, a lot of their definitions are based solely upon the clothing a person wears.

Violence is everywhere, even on the internet. I occasionally watch with sadness as some people, attempting to exhibit their superiority, attack others. Their weapon is their more advance command of a particular website or a more defined desire to hurt others. But, violence is violence, wherever it takes place. And, it is only the small-minded who seek to gain from its unleashing.

Violence is sad. Violence, at any level, hurts. If you've felt it – if you know someone who has been a victim – it is all just sad.

There has always been violence. There probably always will be violence. But, that does not make it right.

People call up all kinds of nonsense to justify their violence. *"It was their karma. They deserved it. Their religion is wrong and against god. I don't like them."*

Whatever the motivation, the outcome is the same – suffering. Whatever the motivation, the sourcepoint is the same, someone's desire to overpower someone else in order to feel better about themselves. But, at the end of the day, who has the right to do anything to anybody? Violence is just wrong.

Do something good. Do something right. And, the whole world will thank you for it. No one thanks anybody for violence.

Speculation

Have you ever noticed that when you are going into a new or different situation that your minds wanders to the place where it plays out the different scenarios of what may or may not happen?

The term, *"May not,"* is usually the best appraisal of what will occur, because what you mind fantasizes about generally never takes place. This is predominately due to the fact that there are other people involved in the, *"What is coming next."* And, each of those people brings their own ideologies and their own desired outcomes to the encounter.

We each do this. We each speculate. Some of us more than others.

Think about it... How many times when you were going to meet a person did you play out the conversation that would take place in your mind? How many times when you were going to meet a person did you think about and envision how that particular situation would be lived and would then guide the next set of events in motion. You probably had it all thought out – the what would happen next. But, it was all in your own mind.

Most of the events of our lives we allow to simply happen – one occurrence to the next. But then, there are events that we are more consciously forced to anticipate. These may be first meetings, meetings with people we care about, meetings with people we don't like, dates, employment events, classes, seminars, places where we must give a speech, whatever... These we think about. We speculate how they will unfold.

From your own life experience, ask yourself, *"How many of these life-events, that your speculated about, turned out anywhere near the way you had thought that they would?"* For most of us, the answer would be few to none. But, the events did unfold. We did live them. They just did not occur they way we had anticipated.

In the spectrum of consciousness, this is a very good lesson. Though we are all probably going to continue to speculate, we should learn to not be defined by our speculations. From this, we enter into a new level of life freedom, where people are as they are, events are as they are – we encounter them, but are not let down when our desire for a specific outcome is not met.

Personal Impact

You know, whenever you discuss the subject of, *"Personal Impact,"* or what impact a person is having on the world around them, you are immediately seen as a hippie or something. And, I'm with you... Hippies should really pull themselves into the twenty-first century. The 60s were great but they ain't ever comin' back...

I remember back when there was a lot of talk about how the earth's ozone layer was being depleted by the use of spray cans. I was at my friend's apartment in Hollywood one day when he was spraying and spraying. I mentioned it to him. He exclaimed, *"I'll be dead anyway, who cares!"* And, that is really the attitude of a lot of people. They do what they do, when they want to do it, and forget about the consequences. Who cares! Their needs are being met in a specific moment.

Recently, I was speaking with a filmmaking friend of mine. He was really upset that there were several sites where a movie he made could be downloaded and watched for free. Of course, these kind of sites are all illegal and stuff. But, they exist out there in the netherworld. So, what can you do?

The reason I found this interesting is that this was a guy who used to watch all kinds of stuff on these sites for free. When he was doing it, that was okay. But now, that it was him losing money, it was no-go.

And, this is life... People do whatever they do until it impacts them.

But, the reality is life is, you too will feel the impact. You will pay the price for what you do. You can call it karma, retribution, whatever...

How we live, what we do, what we say, sets a course of events in motion for our life that will catch up with us.

For example, a couple of my close friends have died from lung cancer due to smoking. One was only thirty-two. But, I still see all these young people smoking – thinking that it will never happen to them. And, believe me, I have seen it, that is horrible way to die.

One guy I knew died of prostate cancer at thirty-eight. The guy ate a horrible diet. But, he liked the food he was eating at the time. That was until what he was eating caught up with him. Again, a very bad way to die.

People grab all kinds of things for free on the internet. Some believe all things should be free. The people who commonly say that are the ones who aren't creating anything. Would you work for free? Would you go to your job for free? Probably not. But, when you take things for free on the internet and from other places, you are robbing others of their income. You can be as cavalier about that as you want to be. But, that is fact.

These are just a couple of examples. The point is, what you do sets the world around you in motion. What you think, what you say, what you take, and what you give, sets the next set of events in your life in motion. Ask yourself, *"What are you doing and why?"*

The ultimate question is, *"What is your personal impact on yourself and the world?"* And, *"Are you willing to pay the price for that impact?"*

What Do You Mean By That?

Have you ever been in the middle of a conversation and the person you are speaking with abruptly questions, *"What do you mean by that?"*

Interesting question, because most people simply assume that they know...

Life's conversations are kind of interesting in that they are all dominated by personal interpretations and definitions. Though the words may be the same, each person interprets them differently.

Certainly, we have all said things that we did not mean. Our mind knew what we wanted to say, but the words just came out wrong.

The funny thing about this is, those mistakes in conversations are oftentimes the things people remember the most. You didn't mean it, but you said it... So, it is believed that is actually how you feel or how you define a person or a situation.

The other side of the issue is that people read into what you have to say and define your words by their own distorted perspective. They put their own spin on what you said, even though, in your mind, that is not what you mean at all.

I had one friend who used to truly contemplate what I said. He would sometimes ask me to clarify what I had said days before. On one side of the issue that was nice; at least he cared what I had to say. But, most of the time we ALL just talk. We say what we say and move on. It means nothing...

In terms of spiritual teachers, people always try to understand the, *"True meaning,"* of what they have to say. This is based in the feeling that there must be some deep spiritual truth hidden between the lines of what they have said. Is there? Or, are they like everyone else? They are just thinking about what they are thinking about, so that is what they are speaking of.

Whichever way you want to look at it, words are open to interpretation. People talk, people lie, people say things they don't mean, people try to control other through the use of what they say.

Words... Don't get lost in 'em.

Things Aren't Always What They Seem

First, with the dawning of the ability to read books on your computer and then with the birth of e-readers, ipads, and tablets, there has been a very sad consequence. Namely, many of the great bookstores have fallen by the wayside and have been forced to close their doors. Here in the L.A. area the legendary *Bodhi Tree* bookstore closed, as did *Acres of Books* in Long Beach. And, that is just to name two.

There remains a few bookstores that truly raise the bar for what a bookstore should be. One is in Santa Cruz, *Logos*. Another is in San Francisco, *The Green Apple*.

I don't know... Tablets are great, but call me, *"Old School,"* there is just something really nice about holding a book and actually turning the pages when you read the words...

As an author, I have this system. I only autograph my books, (new or used), that exist in one of the more esoteric bookstores; like the ones previously named. I never sign my books when I see them in the large chain bookstores. There is just something contrived about that.

In any case, I was in *The Green Apple* a week or so ago and I noticed that they had a few of my books on the martial arts on their shelves. They had *Samurai Zen,* one of my books on Hapkido, *The Ki Process,* and *The Warrior is Silent: Martial Arts and the Spiritual Path.* So, what I was to do? I had to sign them...

Over my shoulder, I noticed that there was an employee stocking the shelves with new reading material. I thought nothing of it.

The moment I disconnected my pen from the small notebook I forever carry in my sport coat pocket, pulled a copy of *Samurai Zen* off the shelf, and begin to sign it, I hear the upstairs telephone ring. I immediate had a feeling...

The employee picked up the phone. He looked over at me. He had been informed what I was doing. *The Green Apple* had put new, in-store cameras in place. He walked over and confronted me.

"Look, its me!" I showed him the cover. With that, he smiled. He didn't know what to do. He went downstairs...

I signed my books. Looked around in the eastern philosophy section but found nothing that caught my eye. I moved downstairs, grabbed my lady who was browsing the art book section, and as we moved towards the door; en-route, I stopped to investigate the store's, behind glass, rare book selection. I heard the people behind the counter speaking...

They didn't realize I was standing there, as they discussed what had occurred upstairs. The manager exclaimed, *"Things aren't always what they seem."*

I smiled. No they are not.

You're Either Doing Something Positive or You're Doing Something Negative. But, which is which?

The fact of life is, we each set our destinies on a course and we are either going to do something positive or we are going to do something negative with our lives. Certainly, there are a million variants within both of those extremes. And, we each do both positive and negative things in our Life-Time. But, there is the course, either positive or negative, that we set ourselves upon and then we continually return to that path. That path, which is decided upon totally by you, is what defines who you are and how you will be remembered in this place we call, *"Life."*

There is a lot of negativity in the world. Sometimes it is very obvious. Other times it is much more subtle. There are those people who hate and criticize everything. Yet, they do nothing positive or creative with their own life.

There is also the armchair quarterback. It is very easy to sit and watch T.V. and believe that you could play the football game better than the players and judge it better than the referee. But, you do nothing to get on the field and actually prove that you can play the game.

It is kind of like the German term, *"Schadenfreude,"* where people take pleasure in other people's misery. Do you do that? A lot of people do.

You know what is or isn't negative. The simple equitation is, "Is what you are doing or saying taking something away from another person or is what you are doing or saying going to affect another person or person(s) in a negative manner?"

The other side of the issue is those who thrive on positivity. They see the best in everyone and everything. Though people who embrace this mindset sometimes come off as naive. Who would you rather be around?

Negativity, criticism, hating the world, or whatever you want to call it, is a developed trait. Yes, we are each born with a personality, then we are shaped by our socioeconomic and cultural environment, but then it is us who chooses to do what we do with those formative factors.

The problem is, so many people are so dissatisfied with their own lives that they are attracted to the dark side. They prefer to embrace the negativity rather than working towards making their own life and the world a better place. This attitude is the sourcepoint for those who follow cult leaders who preach death and destruction, (and/or anything else negative).

It is very simple to make the choice to be positive. If you catch yourself being critical or negative; stop it! Don't make excuses for why you are doing what you are doing. Negative is negative.

Though being positive may take a little more work – especially in this crazy modern world we live in where we are bombarded by the power hungry people attempting to overpower us at every turn. You can be positive.

If you make positivity a part of you, if you catch yourself and shift your mindset whenever you are feeling critical or negative, if you stop making excuses for doing what you do – positivity will emerge.

A previous asked, *"Who would you rather be around?"* A person who is passionate about positivity or a negative being? The answer is pretty obvious. BE the person you would like to BE around.

My Air Conditioner is Broken!

I was driving around this past weekend and the air conditioner in my car decided to stop working. Though the air conditioner fan was turning, it was blowing hot air.

Now, even though I was born in L.A., I am one of those people who hate the heat and avoid the sun at all costs. So, I was not happy with this occurrence.

On Monday, I had to head up to Hollywood. I got in my car and the air condition was again working fine. Then, on my way home, I get on the 101 South and there is a massive traffic jam, and my air conditioner quits working again. I hate the heat! I hate traffic jams! And, I am stuck!

When I finally get home I drop my car of at the mechanic. An hour or two later I get a call. *"Your air condition is fine. It works great. It's not leaking and the motor has no problems. In fact, it got so cold in your car when I was testing it I had to get out to warm up."* But... He had no answers to my question, *"Why did it stop working in the first place?"* I picked up the car and drove off.

Yesterday, the air condition worked fine again. I hoped it was magically fixed. It was not. Today, it died again. I took it to another mechanic. I left the car. An hour later he calls me, *"It's fine, there's nothing wrong with it!"* But... He too had no answers.

You know, this is like life... Sometimes things are just wrong and no one else gets it. No one else experiences it. So, they don't know what to do to fix it. Me too... I don't know what to do. How do you fix what no one believes is broken?

On Your Own

When I was growing up it was the burning desire that the moment you graduated high school and turned eighteen you would get out from under your parent's roof and live out on your own. The few who didn't do this were basically the ones who fathers had bailed and thus they had to take over the roll of the financial caregiver for the family. Today, this desire to be out, on your own, does not seem to be so much the case.

On T.V. and in the movies there is frequently the stereotypical character presented of the geek, gamer, or whatever who lives in their parent's basement and never plans to leave. No doubt, there are a million reasons why a person of adult age does not get out on their own. And certainly, the U.S. economy and the job market have taken a hit in recent years. There is, nonetheless, one simply reality... If you are not out on your own, you are living a sheltered existence and have little understanding of the realities of what to take to actually make it in life.

I have noticed in recent years that many of the people that live under their parent's roof truly attempt to broadcast themselves as, (for lack of a better word), adults. I don't know, maybe they do this as some sort of psychological compensation. But, this is not the case. Though the number of years to adulthood may have been lived, there is little sense that this type of person projects a true understanding of what it takes to survive. Thus, how can they be considered an adult?

Now, I am not saying that leaving the shelter of your parent's house is the end-all to prove you are an adult. Certainly not. But, if you do not have to earn the money, budget it, and then find a way to spend it appropriately and survive, you are presenting a true lacking in the overall development of what being an adult actually is.

I am certain that some of those, who still live under their parent's roof, are going into all kinds of mental debate while reading that statement and pulling up all kinds of alternative explanations. It may even piss some people off. But, that is not the intention. The fact of the matter is, the statement is not made as a judgment. But, it is made as an observation of fact.

If you are not taking care of yourself, financing your own existence, than how can you claim adulthood? And, living independently, away from your parents, is one of the key signs of this. If this is not the case, how can you claim to be anything? If you are not taking care of your own life, at the most basic level, than who and what are you?

I believe people need to think about this as they chart their life into their later, post adolescent, years. Are you and adult? Are you own your own?

When I Was Young...

If I can borrow the title from the Eric Burdon and The Animals song, *"When I was Young,"* as it sets the stage quite well. Actually, it is also a very good song. Take a listen to it if you haven't heard it.

Anyway... You know, when I was young I lived in Hollywood. Hollywood has always been a magnet for creative types. Some have made it in their game of choice, most have not.

I allude to this in one of the early pieces in my book of prose, On the Hard Edge of Hollywood. I was surround by... Well, if I can quote myself,

...no one to talk to
except the dreamers
with no passion left to feel
too old to know that it was too late
too late to be left alive
eleven years old
I walked among them
the hippies and the old poets...

Anyway, there were a lot of creative types around me when I grew up...

I even hung out with Buk, Charles Bukowski, for a bit before he moved to Pedro. I lived about a block and a half from him when he lived on De Longpre and I lived on Hobart.

I met him one day at the supermarket that lay between our two apartments. He was buying some cheap wine and whiskey and I made a joke about it. He invited me over. I think he and his friends were amused at a teenager who could actually throw back whiskey.

Actually, at the time I didn't even know, he was to become what he was to become. Back then, he wrote a column for this local newspaper where he described sexual encounters. As I was about thirteen or fourteen, I thought it was pretty interesting. But, a poet and a literary genius, I had not idea... He never talked about it. All his friends and he discussed was chicks, how much they hated their jobs, and whatever other nonsense came to mind.

I actually didn't hang out there very often. I grew up hanging with a very complex crew of hippies, holies, bikers, hard-livers, and other people living their lives on the edge. Most of them were much older than me. I learned a lot...

I obviously had very little parental supervision growing up. I could pretty much do anything I wanted.

As for Buk, his place was a mess and it smelled like old cigarettes and sometimes barf. Plus, he had a weird crew of people around him. It just didn't draw me in.

The funny thing is, I didn't even discover his poetry and literature until the mid-1970s. Prior to that I had been into the poetry of James Douglas Morrison, Patti Smith, Rimbaud, Ferlinghetti, Kerouac, Ginsberg, and Burroughs. But, when I stated reading his stuff, it really touched me because, through it embraced a different era of time, I could really relate to his literary environment – as that is where I had come up, as well. In fact, when I decided to have another go at grad school, a portion of my thesis discussed his work.

The point of all this is based in the fact that people become who they are from a combination of what they hope to become, where they grow up, and who they associate with. In some cases, people hate where they grow up, so they have to leave it as soon as possible. This is what draws many people to places like Hollywood – the illusion of the ability to become what you dream. And, in some cases, people do become what they hope to become. But, most do not. Most, are left with a lost desire to be something more or are simply completely destroyed.

But, what is more? Most people when they find it, don't even like it. It wasn't what they expected. Or, they want even more of the more. The more they originally thought they wanted was not enough.

Though we are shaped by our environments and our interactions, it is only ourselves who can decide what we do with those influences.

Pursuit always leads to unfulfillment. Because obtainment only equals the desire for more obtainment.

Can you desire to be fulfilled with where you are and what you have? It is hard. But, if you can, then you are free.

As you have created nothing, no one can criticize it. As you have not attempted to become more, you have achieved nothing. Thus, you have surpassed no one and you make no enemies – so you don't have to fight. As the *Tao Te Ching* says, *"For the man of the world, every day something is gained. For the man of Tao, every day something is lost."*

Listen To How You Walk

If you ever want to gain immediate insight into an individual's personality, listen to how they walk. Are their steps quiet and precise or do they stomp across the floor? This tells you a lot about a person.

How do you walk?

Have you ever even taken the time to ponder that question?

If you walk quietly, you are confident and secure within yourself. If, on the other hand, you stomp up stairs and stomp across the floor, you are attempting to bring attention to yourself. Here, look at me! I need your attention.

In the martial arts practitioners are trained in the ability of exact footing placement. As each move you make, each technique you perform, must be very exact – all step are made consciously.

Walking softly is refinement. Walking hard and deliberate, is not.

Who are you? What do you want to portray?

Life: Love or Hate

I was cruising home this afternoon after having taken a moment at Starbucks. I pull up the to stoplight. There was this little curly haired blonde girl hanging her head out of a black SUV. She kind of reminded me of a dog in the way in which she had her head cocked to the side as it rested on the slightly elevated glass of the rear passenger side window of the car. She was maybe eight years old.

She looked at me. I looked at her and smiled. I always smile at everybody...

The light changed. Her car pulled away. As soon as it did, she stuck her tongue out at me.

The funny thing was, it was a really long tongue, like Gene Simmons.

She left her tongue extended all the way up the hill until we reached the next stop sign. There, she looked at the driver whose car was in front of me. He was going straight. I was turning right. The two vehicles took off. I see her stick out her tongue again. She had found a new target.

Life is amusing... We all make our statements. We all want to let people know what we think of them. Some people love people. Some people don't. This is life. Welcome to it...

Soma

There is a certain Bohemianism associated with *eatin'* bad and *drinkin'* hard.

Certainly, for those of us who walk the path of consciousness, there is an enlightenment that can be experienced in these realms. But, it is only for the very few.

Here in L.A.; for the eats, there is *The Pantry,* downtown, *Tommy's,* in Rampart, *Canter's* on Fairfax, *Denny's* on Sunset. But, you can't go to these places during the day. For then, they are overrun by the tourists, the families, and the cellphone picture takers. But, deep in the night, they promise a mysticism. A mysticism that can only be experienced by those who know how to delve into the subtle realms of consciousness.

But, many have faded... There was *Jay Burgers,* over in East Hollywood; right off of Virgil and Santa Monica. 2:00 AM mysticism in the making... I arrived there in the deep, late night, many-many times... I even saw a guy gettin' blow'n away, sitting right next to be, as the clock approached 4:00 AM. That was many-many years ago. But me, being who I am, I did mention *Jay Burgers* in a couple of pieces of literature and I did film a few Zen Films there. As such and so... It is cast to immortality.

As for the drink... And, those of us who partake of its essence. The soma flows free in certain off-the-map locations in L.A.

Now, PC, *"Political Correctness,"* has taken hold of society. As such and because of, many places have shut down. One, for example, *The Escape Room* on 3rd Street. A holy haven... I spend more than a few hours there. I filmed a movie or two within its walls. But, it is gone.

There still are a few, however... A few places remaining, where the dreamer can buy a passageway into the realms of the abyss. *Good Luck Bar,* just off of Sunset. *Ye Rustic Inn* on Hillhurst. *Hinano's,* down Venice way. These are places where the dark, the lost, the poets, and the mystics find their passageway into the ethereal dimensions.

All this being said and stated... Though many desire to eat/drink in these spaces and experience the Bohemianism. Few can actually touch their essence. As few know how to step – one step over the line... Fewer still, actually desire submersion into the abstract realms of soma based enlightenment.

Soma... A passageway to *Nirvana.*

The Impact That You're Having

Most people pass through their life never thinking about the impact that they are having on others or the world around them. They are simply focused upon the fact of how they feel in a particular moment. If they feel good, all is well with the world. If not, look out!

On the spiritual path the zealot is guided to look deeply within themselves and to question why they do what they do. They are guided to take the focus off of self and to do good things for other people. This is very good training that most people never think about pursuing.

One of my primary teachers, Swami Satchidananda, used to talk about love and relationships. He would say, *"Love is like doing business... 'I love you honey. Oh, honey, I love you too.' But then, 'I don't love you anymore. Then, I don't love you either!'"*

Life and its interactions are really a lot like that. If you are being treated the way you want to be treated – If you believe someone likes or loves you, then you are nice to them. If not, look out!

But, the reality of life is... From the smallest interpersonal interactions to the larger goal of trying to help all of humanity, what you say and what you do impacts everyone and everything. What you say and do starts with you. From there, it spreads to the next person and the next, till it reaches around the globe.

As it does start with you. What impact are you having? Are you doing good positive things or not? Are you basing your actions and reactions upon a self motivated point of view or are you trying to add to the greater good of the world?

All life beings with you. What impact are you having?

Momentary Reality

I always find it interesting in life how WE get so locked into the momentary reality of our lives. And, not in a good way. Not in the spiritual way of being in a natural state in the NOW. No, it is much more emotion and ego based.

Periodically in life, most people enter into a space that is overwhelmingly based in emotion. This is commonly due to the fact that either something great has happened so they are filled with an overwhelming sense of self-worth or something they don't like has occurred and they are all encompassed with being upset.

This is a condition of life. Most people do.

In fact, when these sources of emotional life occur one of two events commonly rise out from it.

1. The person who is feeling it attempts to drag as many people into their life-situation as possible. From this, they experience a sense of power and command over others, as they are directing their action.

2. In other cases, people who aren't even the person that is actually experiencing what is happening choose to become engulfed with the feelings and the sensations of the other person simple so that they get that adrenal rush. From this, the two or more of them can keep escalating their feelings be they positive or negative by bouncing their perspectives back and forth.

Though this is a common condition of life, this is where the path of consciousness comes into play. Because those who choose to walk the path of consciousness, the spiritual path if you will, at least try to not be guided and defined by emotion. The reason for this is that emotions, particularly strong ones, are very temporary. Though they are temporary, they are very addictive. This is why you see people out there who are continually falling in and out of love, attempting to argue and cause controversy wherever they go, and so on. They do this, because they have come to find that when something extremely positive or negative is going on, they feel ALIVE – they feel they have power, they feel they have a purpose.

Another factor related to this is that power, like emotion, is temporary. Power, like emotion, is based in ego. Therefore any situation based in the power of emotion is ruled and defined by one specific mindset, one person. Therefore they are the one in control. And, if they are in control, they are the one to set the tone of the moment. So, others are simply following their lead. They are not being in control of their own life and life-time. This is where mod mentality is born – being a part of something to get a boost of that adrenalized energy. And, we have all see the bad things that rise from mob mentality.

Ultimately, emotion is based in a specific person's appraisal of a specific situation in a given moment in time. For example, what may make one person feel great will make another person feel very bad. So, there is no commonality to emotion. Why? Because emotion is based in personal definition. Emotion is based in ego. Emotion is based in like and dislike. I am, you are not. You are, I am not. I like this, you do not. You like that, I do not.

The problem with emotion is that people do a lot of bad things based in it. All anyone has to do is look, not only at themselves, but at the whole evolution of human and view the things that were done, based in emotion, that later people were very sorry about.

Though action(s) taken in a moment of emotion may seem very right and empowering in that moment – actions enacted due to emotion are the ones that most commonly will later be seen to have actually damaged the evolution of your life.

The ultimate understanding is, Reality is Momentary. What you feel now, you will not feel in a few moments. The things you think are all so important now, will not matter in a few days or weeks. Who you see yourself as now, will change. The things that empowered you now and you take action on, may very well come back to haunt you later in life. With this as a basis of understanding, it can be concluded, it is far better to let the emotions of the moment be noticed, even experienced, but never allowed to control who and what you truly are.

Ultimately tomorrow is based upon what you do today. If you seek a life defined by emotional upheaval, then you will always be chasing the high of emotion. If you seek a life based in peace, and a future not defined by things down yesterday, you choose to not be dominated and control by your emotions and the emotions of others. From this, you becomes free, because emotions will not dominate you. You will see any emotion for what it is, *Momentary Reality.*

Nobody Wants to Die

Nobody wants to die. Even people who take their own life simply wish that their life were better.

The reality of life is, we are all going to die. That is simply the definition of this existence. There are all kinds of religious beliefs in the hereafter, reincarnation, and other realms and plains, but here is the fact; you, in this body, will not be here forever.

Some people decide it is time for them to leave their body before they die of natural or unnatural causes. There is no right or wrong with this. Those who make these distinctions are simply basing their judgments upon religious and cultural beliefs that are programmed into their mind and are not organic. Those who do want to die want to do so to escape the pain of life they are feeling due to age, physical disease, emotional instability, physical or psychological abuse, lack of desire fulfillment, or whatever... But, the reality of this is, they would not want to die if their life was better, different. If they getting what they wanted out of life, they would not choose to leave it.

Then, there are the people who are handed a death-sentence from disease and they fight and fight to stay alive going through all kinds of pain and suffering but they still do not wish to give up on life. They too wish that life were better. But, for whatever psychological motivation they choose to not leave. Again, this is not more right or better, it is simply the bases of who they are.

As our life goes on, we will all encounter the death of others. In some cases it will be the death of people we truly care about.

From a personal perspective, I have witnessed death from a very young age. I remember back to Christmas Eve when I was three. My grandfather had become ill and we went to the hospitable and I clearly remember how we spent the night there in the waiting room until my father emerged telling us of his passing in the hour morning hours. We then went home and I found it very stage to be opening Christmas gifts. But, that was simply my parent's way to give me some stability.

My father died when I was ten from a massive heart attack. He was only in his forties. So, we never saw it coming. I remember his friend from work coming to our door in tears, as he had been on the job when he passed away.

In each case, with the death of each person, you are left without him or her. The living is the one holding the memory. The person who dies is no longer in the physical equation.

Life equals death. What we do in the short period of time is all we have that will define us.

Where is Knowledge Based?

For those of you who know me, you know that I have been a vintage guitar aficionado since way back in high school. I have always admired the craftsmanship of aging instruments. As such, I have developed quite a base of knowledge on the subject.

Again, for those of you who know me, you know that as a life-distraction, I enjoy going to places like thrift stores, antique shops, and swap meets, because you never know what type of interesting cultural memorabilia you may find in those locations.

With this as an introduction, today I went into a local thrift store. Inside the boutique section of the store I noticed that they had a very cheaply made *Rickenbacker 4001* bass imitation. It had a bolt on neck, a cheaply made Rickenbacker headstock plate, and so on. They were asking $600.00 for it. Which would not be a bad price if it were real. It was not. Not even close...

As I was examining it, the manager walked by. As I know him, just a bit, I let him know about the fact that this was not a true *Rickenbacker.* He asked, *"Why?"* I explained it to him. He then got on his walkie-talkie and contacted the guy who had priced the instrument earlier in the morning. The guy told him, *"No. It was very real. It simply had been repainted."* I smiled. *"All you have to do is google image search it,"* I told the manager.

This situation brought an interesting realization to mind. People think they know many things that they do not. They base their facts upon opinions or poorly researched understandings. Where his or her beliefs come from is anybody's guess. And, why they fight so adamantly to protect their beliefs is based who knows what – a million cultural and psychological factors, I guess. But, in many cases in life, people will argue their point of view with you until the day they die. *"I am right! You are wrong!"* This, even if they are totally wrong and you, (or in this case me), are totally right.

This is why I do not engage in conflict. Because it serves no purpose. I just laugh if off.

People have their opinions. Right or wrong, that is their opinion. Arguing with them will never change their mind. In fact, showing them the truth, in many cases does not even change their mind.

Me, I thought to pull up a few images of a true *Rickenbacker 4001* on my phone to the show the manager. But, it's not my store. The guy who priced the instrument is not my employee. And, why cause conflict?

If there is one ultimate logical reason to give credence to those who walk upon the Spiritual Path, it is the fact that they are constantly investigating what they do and why they do it. This is the pathway to *Nirvana* – as living life in this manner reveals the ultimate truth of human nature and thereby revealing the True Self.

Most people do not want to do this. They do not want to live their life like this. It takes a lot of work. This is not to say they are bad and/or less. They are simply doing what they are doing. But, at the end of the day all that we have is the true knowledge of who we are and why we do what we do. And, the only way to gain this knowledge is by removing as many layers of the puzzle of SELF as possible. To do this, you must perform each life-action with a much factually based knowledge as possible and as much psychologically revealed understanding as possible. From this, the layers of

Life-Nonsense are removed and Ultimate Truth is revealed.

Wild in the Streets

I was cruising home a couple of days ago from having an afternoon *latte'* at my local Starbucks. There was a car in front of me in my lane and then one of those smaller black sedan style limos passed us to the right. A little bit farther down the road, the driver of the limo changed lanes and totally cut off the car in front of me. The driver of the car honked their horn. That's a pretty natural response, I think. In any case, the driver of the limo slammed on his breaks and came to a complete stop on the street. I was expecting someone to get out but no one did. They both just sat there in the cars.

I had never seen anything like this before. I've seen a lot of drive-arounds with somebody flipping the other person off and yelling, *"Fuck you."* I've also seen a lot of people get out of their cars and in some cases go to blows. I'm no saint. I've done both myself. But these two drivers did nothing. They just sat there. Finally, with traffic building up behind us, I decided that it was time to stop watching reality unfold. I pulled around the car in front of me and drove on.

I continued looking I my rear-view mirror, however. But, as far as I drove, nothing happened. The two cars just sat there.

The last time I personally encountered a situation something like this, I was in San Francisco. I was driving up a very steep hill and the car in front of me was sightseeing or something. The street was narrow so when they stopped their car to point at something I had no way of going around them. So, I lay onto my horn. The driver, an older man, gets out of his car. I'm in no mood for this so when we walked towards my car I was ready. He says, *"We're tourist..."* I replied, *"This is San Francisco and you don't hold people up on the hills. Get your fucking car out of the way!"* He walked back to his car and drove on.

This encounter made me realize something however. Nothing good was going to come from this confrontational encounter. Yeah, it was the guy in front of me doing something wrong but I was reacting, or overreacting, in not a good way. You know, if you get out and hit somebody, yeah you may have some personal satisfaction, but you go to jail and/or get sued. If you tell 'em off, like I did, that just spoils the other person's experience.

Now, everybody does something wrong when they drive. We all cut people off by mistake. We don't realize someone is behind us or beside us, etc... When I do that, I wave at the person, *"Sorry..."* Some people don't. Some people blame the other person for even existing.

The reality of life is, if you're going to go toe-to-toe with every person who makes some minor mistake in your life, you're going to be fighting all the time. I know it's hard, but if you want to have any inner peace you simply have to embrace forgiveness. You have to let it go... No good ever comes from confrontation.

Know Who You Are

People quote me. I always find it interesting when I go to places on the web and I find that someone has taken a passage from one of my books and pasted it up there. The words are usually taken from books I have written like, *About Peace, Nirvana in a Nutshell, Zen O'clock, Essence: The Zen of Everything,* or *Zen in the Blink of an Eye.*

That's great! If you like the words, if the words help you, quote away...

People also write negative things about me. When I see these comments, the main thing I realize is that they people who are attacking me do not know me, do not understand what I'm about, and they're completely getting everything about me wrong.

But, this is life. People say and do all kinds of things based on their own perception of reality. Some people base their existence on positivity – and on spreading that positivity to others. Some people base their existence upon negativity. Thus, they spread their reality just the same.

This is *yin and yang.* This is life. We each encounter positive and we each encounter negative people in our lives. That's just the way it is.

What we must learn from all of this is that we must know who we are. Because at the root of our existence this is the only place where we can truly embrace ultimate understanding, divine consciousness – enlightenment, if you will.

And, that place of knowing who you are is only in your own being.

We are who we are. We can be negative, but what is the result of that? Or, we can base our reality on positivity. What does that bring about?

The answers are clear. If what you are doing does not make the ALL better, you can change.

Conflict

Conflict. Some people love conflict. I had a friend who used to thrive on conflict. He loved it so much that he would always stir things up. He would tell one person that another person said something that they did not. He would do this just to see what would happen. He would also plant seeds of conflict in people's minds about other people and other situations at every opportunity. I quickly saw through this nonsense and was never drawn into it. Others, as I would witness, were not that astute as to this individual's mindset and they were frequency dawn into conflict, even physical altercations, by this person.

If you ever watch *Reality T.V.* the cast members thrive on conflict. The ones that are the most popular are the ones who create conflict or are always at the center of it. I am sure the producers of these shows want it that way as the show would probably be fairly boring if everyone was simply getting along.

There is a certain adrenaline rush that comes from conflict. When you are in the middle of it your senses are turned on and your blood pressure is up. Some people come to like this. Some people even get addicted to it. Though those who do, for the most part, are completely unaware of the personal motivation for being drawn into it.

I think we can each look to people in our lives that have been addicted to conflict. They are the ones who are angry at a moments notice and are always seeking out the worst in every person and situation.

There are also those who are the source of conflict – those who create it. From creating it, what they find is empowerment. They come to understand that they can actually have control over other people. They do this by the spreading of misinformation, as was the case of previously described friend. From this they find an answer to something that is lacking within themselves. It makes them feel in control – important. This does not make this behavior right; it simply allows them to forget their own inadequacies and emotional pain for the time the conflict is enacted.

People who follow the path of conflict are ultimate defeated by it. Though they will argue to the end that this is and will not be the case. *"I'm an angry person." "I have the right to be mad." "That person is an asshole."* Or, *"That situation is wrong."* These are all common expressions that a person addicted to conflict will use and there are many more.

But, at the end of the day, what does conflict bring you? Though you may have a moment rush adrenaline. That rush will pass. Then, as with any drug, you will be left searching for your next fix. But, more than simply that fact, conflict only creates further conflict.

Conflict is not refined consciousness. It is simply an animalist reaction. Though for the moment you are in you may be filled with energy, it is a negative energy. What comes from negative energy? Negativity. And, negativity is never good.

Walk away from conflict.

What People Believe

It forever dumbfounds me when I hear about what some people believe and what they do because of their beliefs. I mean, how many bad things have been done to other people, (and this world in general), simply because somebody believed something?

Though a particular individual may be very steadfast in their beliefs, that does not necessarily make them right.

When you look at all the carnage that's going on across the planet, it is very sad. And, this is nothing new; it has been going on forever. What is the majority of it based upon? *People's beliefs.*

When you are on the other side of a particular person's or group's beliefs, we each can question, *"Why would somebody do that?"* But, to that person, they're right. They are doing something good, just, and maybe even holy.

Now, here is where it gets complex. A lot of people who do these things do them because they believe what someone or something else is doing is wrong. This can be as simple as wearing the wrong clothing, saying the wrong thing, behaving in a certain manner, or simply being in the wrong place at the wrong time.

But, if you are hurting someone or something that is just not right, no matter what you believe!

Ultimately, life is based upon belief. We all do what we do because we believe what we are doing is right. But, if you step outside of your personal bubble, the next person or the next group will have a totally different set of beliefs than you and they may believe that what we are doing is totally wrong or even unholy.

Complicated? Not really. It is simply a condition of life.

But, there is one very simply rule to follow. No matter what you believe, remember that everybody has his or her own belief. Thus, those beliefs may be different from yours. As such, accept as opposed to attack. Do not make or take on battles. Though your beliefs may drive you to make a statement or throw a blow, remember what you are motivated to do is only based on your belief. They are not a universal truth, as there is no such thing, simply a belief.

Beliefs are a temporary as the life of the person who believes them.

I'm Glad You Know So Much More Than Me. Maybe You Should Be the One Writing the Books.

Every now and then I will receive an email or a letter from someone who has read one of my books and they tell me I am completely wrong. They say that I don't understand spirituality at all. These messages always make me smile because if the person who was contacting me truly understood anything about spirituality, mysticism, or enlightenment they would know that there is not only one path. They would see that each person's path to spirituality and personal enlightenment is unique onto themselves. It is like my teacher Swami Satchidananda used to say, *"Truth is one, paths are many."*

People love to associate themselves with one religion or one teacher. From this, they are allowed to exist in an environment where there is only one message being propagated. For them, there is only one truth. The truth that is being spelled out in whatever religious text or by whatever teacher they follow. For them, right is right and everybody else who follows a different path is wrong.

How many wars throughout history have been fought because one person held a different religious ideal than another?

With the answer to that question as a basis, we should all understand that your way might not be my way, just as my way might not be your way. You may think I am wrong. But, that does not make me wrong. You simply believe that I am wrong. You simply believe that you are right.

Do you see the common factor here? One person thinking and believing one thing.

This goes for me too. I believe, *"To each their own."* I believe, *"Find your own enlightenment and life fulfillment in your own way."* That's just me... But also, I don't go around telling people that they are wrong. I let them live their religious experience and find out their own truth in their own time and in their own way.

Ultimately, we each believe what we believe. Some of us base our beliefs on what we were told or on what we have studied. Others of us base on beliefs on what we have experienced. In either case, it is our understandings and our beliefs that make us who we are.

We are who we are. We believe what we believe. If we can learn from what others have to say, GREAT! But, we can never encounter the ultimate truth through judgment.

As I have written about and discussed in so many ways over the years, judgment is never the path to realization. Judgment is simply a way to pass judgment. It is a means to make yourself feel better, smarter, and more actualized than someone else.

Judgment makes no one right or wrong. It simply makes the person who is passing judgment feel that someone else is wrong and they are right. The ultimate truth of enlightenment is, to experience enlightenment one must forgo judgment and enter into the space of divine acceptance.

The Road You're On

The road you're on is obvious. What you're doing while you're on that road is obvious. What you have to do to stay on that road is obvious. Where that road will lead you is also obvious. Though this is fact, many people pretend that is not the case.

In life, it is very obvious that what you are doing now will lead you to your next set of available circumstances. Many people avoid this fact, which is why so many people end up in a place where they never wanted to exist. Because of this fact, you must ask yourself, *"Is the road you're on leading you to where you want to be?"*

When you ask yourself where you want to ultimately end-up, this is where things get a little bit complicated. Why? Because we all want something from our life. We all want to end-up somewhere. We all want to do what we ultimately what to do. And to get there, we have to take certain actions. But, there is a very big difference between being guided down our life road by ego, desire, and thirst for power, over that of choosing to consciously enter a path and then follow through with what it take to obtain our end-goal.

This is why so many lives become corrupted or end unfulfilled. This is also why so many people are injured by people who do not care what about the affect they are having on others as they are only focused upon their own end-goal.

The fact of life is, if all you are thinking about is yourself and/or how you feel, you road will forever be troubled as you will injure others on your path to self-attainment.

Ask yourself. *"Does what you are doing help me, help others, or both?"* Now, turn off your ego and re-ask yourself the same question. With the ego turned off, the true answer is always self-evident.

Remember, just because you want something does not mean you can or should have it. Wanting is the way of the world. Knowing what you should have is the path of consciousness.

Thinking

When I was an undergraduate at CSUN one of my professors said something very profound. He said, *"It doesn't matter what you get your degree in, what going to college teaches you is how to think."*

I have forever held onto that statement. Not just in terms of why a person should attend a college or university but that you really need to train your mind how to think.

Most people allow their mind to wonder, driven from one desire to the next. Ken Kesey defined this as, *"Current fantasy."*

But, life and living a conscious, good life is much more than this. You can't just let life happen, fueled by momentary desires.

As we all know, the desires we hold today will be different tomorrow. And, the karma enacted by the obtaining of those desires may negatively define our tomorrows.

Because of this we ALL have to think. We have to step-back and take a moment to think. We have to define our thoughts and not just let them rule our existence.

By learning how to think, we discover our own true nature and we can pass though life consciously, as opposed to living an undefined random reality of passing from one emotion and desire onto the next.

Think.

Stand Up For Your Rights

Here in the West and, in fact, in most of the modern world, we are taught that we should each stand up for our rights. From a philosophical perspective, this is a very good concept. But, the fact of the matter is, most people do not understand what standing up for their rights actually means. Most believe that you should simply be able to express your belief that something is your right and all will fall into place in your favor. This, however, is not the case.

To stand up for your rights is not simply your exerting what you believe to be right and true. It also involves you fighting and perhaps being injured while attempting to achieve a goal that may never come to pass.

If we look to lives of the people like Rosa Parks and Martin Luther King Jr., we see that their actions change the United States forever. But, in the process, Martin Luther King Jr. was assassinated. Mahatma Gandhi and all of the people that fought against British Colonialism struggled for years and many were beaten, imprisoned, and even killed for their actions until India finally gained its freedom. Nelson Mandela spent years in prison before Apartheid was defeated. And, these are just a few of the very obvious examples.

Then, there were the movements that did not succeed such as the counterculture revolution that took place in the United States during the 1960s. Here, the people struggled for an idealize world based on love, peace, and individual freedom. During this time period the cops would beat the protestors, cut their hair, and throw them in jail. In some cases these people were killed; i.e. the case that took place at Kent State University. Plus, how many people who survived this onslaught by the authorities were left scared for life?

Standing up for your rights is an idealized concept. We all feel we have rights. We all feel that we can do whatever we feel we want to do. But, that is not the true basis of rights.

If I can look back to a (now) humorous event in my life it may illustrate the understanding of personal rights. When I was a late teenager, going to college, I rented my first apartment not far from the campus. I was also an active musician. So, I would frequently play guitar. There was an older, retired, gentleman living in the apartment below me. Each time I would start to play, I would hear his rumblings. He would mutter inaudible words and eventually cuss at me from below. One night, I had enough. I walked down the stairs empowered with all my rights. I confronted him. It turned into an argument. But, what I soon came to realize, during the argument was that, the problem with me standing up for my rights was that my rights were inflicting on the rights of another person. I wanted to play guitar. But, my guitar playing was taking away this man's desired solitude. So, who was right? Who rights were actually being violated?

There are only personal answers to this question. Defined by personal ideologies. But, it does provide food for thought.

I don't like the term, *"Greater Good,"* because it is most often used to describe one person or one group's desires for a desired outcome. But, the main point is, and this is the question you have to ask yourself before you ever go on a campaign of standing up for your rights, how does standing up for your rights affect others? And, does you standing up for your rights negatively affect the rights of someone else?

Again, that is a philosophic question. But, the answer also defines who you are as a human being. Do you care more about you – your ego and your desires? Or, do you care about other people and humanity in general?

If you actually care about the Greater Good and not only about yourself, then you will question your motivation for standing up for your rights. You must do this, and then you must weight the price that will be paid – not only by your life but what must be paid by the lives of others involved with you. You must do this, and be willing to pay whatever price will be charged, before your ever decide that you should stand up for your rights.

Standing up for your rights is not a simple choice.

The Quality of Sound

The fact of the matter is, the minds of the young follow the trends and from this they guide the minds of the masses. Today, music is listened to by downloading music that was digitally created onto a tablet, pad, or phone and then it is broadcast directly into the ears through mini headphones. That's all good. The music is quick to create and its transportation is very portable. But, the quality of the sound is gone.

Quality of sound is almost impossible to describe to someone who has not developed the ability to understand the difference. But, for those of you who exist in this modern era all you have to do is to go and pick up an unscratched LP that was recorded on analogue recording equipment and then play it on a turntable with a good needle, run through a good amplifier or receiver, (preferable powered with tubes), and played through a good set of speakers. The sound is awesome. There is no other way to say it but it is just better.

Now, I am not one of those people who are simply reminiscing about times gone past. The truth be told, I was one of the first people to embrace the digital era, way back when people would argue that making music with synthesizers was not making music at all. But, as I have lived through a few eras of technology, I can state with some authority what sound better and what sounds worse.

Technology has made music creation much easier and much faster. I was recently watching a documentary about The Who and Pete Townshend described it very well when he discussed how this one riff took them days to create but now it could be done in fifteen minutes.

The reality of life is, all things change. With all change something is lost. When something is lost, soon it is forgotten. When it is forgotten all of the perimeters that made it important do not matter anymore. But, with this loss, sensory aptitude and defined understandings go away, as well. The ultimate truth of life is, when all that is needed is sensory stimulation, better no longer matters.

You Will Not Remember This Moment

The fact of the matter is, you more than likely will not remember this moment.

Remembering is a condition of life. Forgetting is also a condition of life. Most moments – most things you do; you will not remember.

The only time things become memorable is when they strike a point/a place in you where something is touched. Your senses are stirred and that moment is cast to memory. The majority of the moments of you life are, however, lived and then forgotten.

From a spiritual perspective, many ascetic traditions believe that you should live a life void of stimuli. You should simply live in a space of non-involvement, away from wordily affairs and, instead, focus your life upon your own inner meditation. As memories are not created, the mind is not bound to them. For some, this is their calling. For most, it is not.

On the other side of the coin, the way of the world teaches that you must DO, you must EXPERIENCE – you must HAVE to live a fulfilled life. Most follow this path. The problem with this path is, however, there is always something bigger, something more to do. So, those who walk down this road generally end up unfulfilled. This is combined with the fact that this path is fueled by adrenaline. As such, the adrenaline becomes a drug. When it is not being embraced there is a sense of loss.

This path is based upon emotion and stimuli. Though things may become more memorable, there is always a sense of fulfillment.

Many are driven through life fueled simply my momentary, unchecked, emotions. *"I want this." "I want that." "I want to feel this way." "I want that person to feel the way I want them to feel." "I want revenge."* And, so on…

The problem with living life on this level is that you are out of control. You are not in control of what is going on in your life. You have no focus and, as such, life is dominated by random emotions and desires. From this, nothing is ever achieved except the possible momentary fulfillment of those emotions and desires. Thus, when you get to the end of your life you will have nothing to show for it. You will look back to memories and what will they be?

You have to ask yourself, when you are doing the small things, (and the big things in your life), *"At the end of the day, what do I want to remember?" "What memories will fill my mind when I look back to them?"*

Your life. Your choice.

Knowing What You Don't Know

I always find it very amusing when someone who has no idea about how the independent film industry actually works tells me how I should be doing something or that am I doing something totally wrong.

Over the many years I have been involved in the film industry I have received messages telling me how virtually everything I have done is wrong. These messages generally come from someone who has never made a film and most likely never will.

It all began when Donald G. Jackson and I were making *the Roller Blade Seven.* Don and I knew we wanted to create something very different. We initially hired an editor to help us create our vision when we had completed the filming process of the movie. The man edited the movie for us for a couple of days with Don and I guiding his every action. But, he didn't get it. He took Don off into another room one day and told him, *"You are really pushing the envelope too far."* When Don relayed his message to me with both laughed. We knew exactly what we were doing. And, as I have previously mentioned in my writings on the movie, the mistake this editor made was that he taught me how to use the equipment. We were gone. We rented an editing suit. I became the editor. And, we took the movie to the level we hoped it would reach.

We must have done something right. People are still talking (and criticizing) the film over twenty years later. In fact, most of the people who are criticizing this movie were not even born when we made it.

People also have told me that Zen Filmmaking is all-wrong. Wrong? How can anything be wrong when the entire premise of Zen Filmmaking is based upon the concept that there are no mistakes? But, I won't get all-philosophical on you here...

People also have contacted me detailing that my story structures are all-wrong. Again, to understand my filmmaking style you must understand that I don't care about stories. The stories have all been told. I care about visional images, with occasional dialogue, taking the viewer on a mind-ride. The fact of the matter is, most people have only seen my most talked about films. They never go and investigate all my other work.

Some of my films actually have defined storylines. Can you believe it?

Also, I have heard random comments about the fact that I don't pay actors. First of all, that is not true. For actors who bring no name value to a film I may not pay them in cash. But, I do pay them in other ways. I give them a chance to be in a film that will be completed and will be distributed – which is not the case of many independent films. During their time on the set they get hone their acting skills for the camera. Plus, they get to have a film, (a calling card), that they can show to their family, friends, agent, and the world.

For only asking a few hours of their life, I think that is quite a nice payment.

Hell, the entire time we were making *the Roller Blade Seven,* which took month-upon-months, I got paid virtually nothing in terms of cash. But, at the end of the day, I was happy to have donated my time. And, in the early stages of my career, I acted in several films where I was not paid.

In fact, this is the case with most of the low-budget, independent film industry. The cast and the crew are not paid in money.

But you see, people don't know these facts. People who watch films, particularly independent films, want to armchair quarterback the production. As has long been the case, my suggestion to everyone is, before you throw in your two cents about something that you know nothing about, why don't you go and make your own movie.

Alone or Together

I guess it is appropriate that I discuss relationships on Valentines Day.

There is this unexplained innate desire and understanding throughout all cultures that people need to be in a relationship. I am not even going to go into the whys and wherefores of that. We will just assume that it seems to be human nature. As such, everybody appears to be seeking just that, a relationship. Some find it. Some do not.

I was having a discussion with this one friend of mine on the phone a few years ago. I was detailing that this one mutual person we knew was meeting women via this dating service on the Internet. As my friend was without a mate, I told him he should go to that site. *"I don't want to meet a girl. I want to be a star!"* He exclaimed. As we met via the film industry, this was a very funny statement.

Some people want to be alone. They have been through bad relationships or they just have another focus in their life. That's their choice. Most people are not like this, however.

Others try-and-try to find love but it eludes them. For example, the person I was referencing in the phone conversation decided it was time for him to find a woman. He would often detail how he had previously been very-involved with this one girl. But, he blew her off. Once she had moved on, he realized his folly. He went back to her in tears but it was too late, she had found someone else. Much later, he had found this Internet service and he was exchanging e-mails and then meeting women for coffee. If they liked each other, he would take things farther.

Finally, he met this one woman. All was working out well. He liked her, she like him. She wanted to take the relationship to the next level. But, he blew her off. He followed the exact same path as he had done before. He later called me and was very dismayed at his decision. *"But, she wasn't enough like my mother,"* he stated.

You see, people follow patterns. People find all kinds of reasons to bail from relationships if that is what they do. In his case, he had a mother issue. Some men really love their mothers; others hate them. This all defines who a person is and who they will be in a relationship.

Then, there is the other side of the issue, one person wanting to be in a relationship and the other person not being willing to commit. Yet, one of the two hangs on-and-on. In my younger years, I encountered a couple of woman who just would not take the hint. They were each very nice girls, but they did not offer me want I was looking for. But, they latched on and would not go away. This led me to do all kinds of dastardly deeds in order to get them to move on. But still, they would not go.

This is the other side of relationships. One person wants it and one person does not.

No matter how much you may love someone, you have to be willing to view an individual for who they truly are and what are their actual needs. If you can't meet those needs, stop trying to throw yourself at them, for all this does is to damage both of your lives.

It is kind of like when you are young and believe if you find love all things in the universe will fall into place. You will be happy forever and ALL will be taken care of. If you're older, you can look back and smile at that appraisal of life. If you're still young and believe those ideologies, look forward to a rude awakening.

Some people are very lucky and they meet the right person very young. I have known people that actually met in junior high school and have stayed together forever. That is very cool. Unusually, but cool... Most of us dance around for a long time before we meet the right person. That's not bad or good, that's just modern life. Certainly, I've detailed the craziness of my interpersonal interactions in my novels and poetry. That was simply my path.

And, this is the thing... We each dance around, we meet people, we do what we do, and then it either lasts, or we end it – sometimes badly. The thing is, in your quest, you have to remain conscious. Many people are looking for love to the degree that they throw consciousness out of the window, as their only quest is companionship. This leads to mistakes and other bad things.

I mean, we always hear about people being scammed and lied to on the Internet. Be careful!

I can tell you from personal experience if you travel to foreign lands and believe you have found perfect love, again be careful! As their will undoubtedly be a language barrier, even if you both can communicate with a mutual language – different cultures have different attributes and if you are not from that culture it is very hard to see the subtleties. I know this from personal experience. So, be careful!

Ultimately, if you want to be with someone, at the end of the day, you have to understand that everybody has faults. No one will be that perfect, idealized image of love you have envisioned. And mostly, if you want to remain in a relationship, you have to forgive. Everybody does wrong things. Where is your forgiveness meter set at?

But, love is great. I recommended it. Be in love.

My Way or the Highway

In life you come across many people that believe that they know the right way – that there way is the only way. *"My way or the highway..."* As the old saying goes.

In business environments this is often the necessary evil. The buck stops here. So, there must be the infrastructure for one person to be in charge.

Too many cooks in the kitchen often mess up the progression of a desired outcome when everyone is throwing in their opinion. So, there needs to be one captain of the ship – one person in charge.

But, then we get to life. Many people want ALL-THINGS to only be done their way. If someone disagrees with them or if someone takes the side of any person with an opposing view, then that person is history.

This, my way or the highway, attitude towards life is based upon all kinds of things. None of them are good.

Maybe the person is insecure. Maybe they are power hungry and this is the only way for them to achieve power – by forcing their views onto others and, thus, making others do as they say. Maybe they were held down and repressed by their family or their job. Whatever the cause, they have bought into the Life-Lie that they are right and others are wrong.

There is no right and wrong. There is only your opinion of what is right and wrong. Which is all fine and good. We all have our opinions. Where this concept goes haywire is when you try to force your mindset on others.

The next time someone says, *"My way or the highway,"* say, *"See ya..."* 'Cause you don't want to hang out with a person like that anyway.

You Talk Too Loud

In the evening I like to take a moment, sit outside with a glass of wine or a cup of tea, look out over the ocean, and watch the sunset. I've been doing this for years but recently I've had a new next-door neighbor move in. I was sitting outside last night. He apparently got a phone call. He walks up to his open window and begins to speak LOUDLY. Something he does far too frequently. He was having this whole conversation about what, I guess, he does for a living. He was so loud. The conversation was so annoying. The spirituality was so robbed from the moment that I was forced to go inside before the sun had set and close my windows and door.

I think we all have experienced situations such as these where someone is having a loud conversation and they are doing it so someone else can hear.

Are they doing it to impress the other person with what they have to say? Maybe.

Are they doing it to claim space – take over the energy of a space? Maybe.

Are they doing it because they think they have something worth saying that someone else should hear? Maybe.

Are they doing it to be annoying? Possibly.

Are they doing it because they are inconsiderate? Obviously.

This happens to everybody. I remember back to an episode of the show, *The Osbourne's*. This was one of the early Reality T.V. shows that followed the trials and tribulation of the family of rock star, Ozzy Osbourne. They lived in this massive custom build house. Yet, the next-door neighbors were talking loudly late into the night and disturbing them so much that Ozzy threw something over the fence, breaking a glass table or something...

There is also another situation that relates to this that I find interesting. That is when you are somewhere, in some public place, and someone decides that you need to hear the conversation that they are having. A couple examples come to mind.

I was having breakfast in this restaurant in Vegas a couple of years ago. I pull out my phone, which was a Blackberry at the time, to check my email. This twenty-something girl, sitting at the table next to us with her parents, notices what I am doing. She immediately beings to speak loudly. *"Oh, the new iPhones are the best phones out there. They are so much better than the Blackberry."* I smiled to myself. *"Like I need your opinion..."*

Another time; and this goes back deep – maybe thirty years. I was in this restaurant with my girlfriend and the minute we sit down, the guy at the table next to us begins to raise the loudness of his conversation. *"I used to have long hair. But, I started to lose my hair so I cut it. Any man who has long hair is going to go bald."* Yeah right, buddy. I had long hair then and I still have long hair now and my hairline hasn't changed. It's not long hair that does or does not make a man go bald.

On the other side of the issue I was having a pseudo-production meeting at a restaurant with a friend of mine. We were going to produce a movie together and we invited a possible cameraman to have lunch with us. We were talking about the project. This guys comes over to us and says, *"Could you keep it down, your conversation is really bothering me."*

Now, this was a very large, very crowded, very noisy restaurant. And, for whatever reason, this guy was honing in on our conversation from several tables away.

My friend, who is a street-savvy guy like myself and I look at each. Before one of us could tell the guy to F-off the cameraman says, *"Oh sure. Sorry."* My friend exclaims to me, *"The voice of reason..."*

The reality is, and I think this is the case for all of us; we don't want to hear what someone else has to say when we don't want to hear it. This is especially the case when what they are saying, the volume they are talking, is invading our space.

For those of us who live, particularly in the city, this whole experience is based on the too many rats in a cage syndrome. But, what can be done? I don't really have an answer. To confront someone every time one of these situations occurs would only cause ongoing confrontations. And, that makes life even worse. Worse... Based on what someone else has inconsiderately instigated.

But, damn, I wish people would just shut-up and keep what they have to say to themselves.

Liar

Whenever I teach a class on filmmaking I begin by educating the students on the number one rule of filmmaking; which is, *"Everybody lies."*

Lying is prevalent throughout all aspects of the film industry. But, I won't go into that here. If you are interested you can read my book, Zen Filmmaking, to find out more about that subject.

But here, we get to life… Think about it; is there any one of us who has not lied at one time or another in our life? I think not. In fact, a recent court ruling stated, in essence, that lying is just a part of life.

But, what does lying do to relationships and personal interactions? What it does is make them based upon falsity and deception. And, some people lie all the time!

I remember back to this one girl I knew who I eventually discovered was a pathologic liar. She lied about everything. And, I mean everything! When I confronted her about this, her statement was, *"I was just frontin'…"*

That's it! That's all you have to say about all the lies you told!

Most people are not that pathological, however. But, if you ask them, they will each have a reason for why they have lied. *"I wanted to obtain something from someone." "I wanted to be liked or loved." "I thought this would make me look like a better, bigger, more important person."* Whatever… There is always a reason or maybe better put an excuse to lie if you allow yourself to walk down that path.

Now, aside from the fact that the lies you tell may catch up with and you will be really embarrassed if you are found out – you really need to think about the impact you are having on other people when they believe your lies. It damages their life. It harms their evolution. It hurts them. Why? Because they believed in YOU and YOU turned out to be based in falsities.

    To keep yourself from developing the need to lie is doable. Not necessarily easy, but doable. What you have to do is you have to be <u>become</u>. Now <u>becoming</u> does not mean that you have to become a zillionaire, a movie star, a star athlete, or a superstar rapper. What it means is that you have to become an ideal example of you. You have to develop a lifestyle where you are comfortable with yourself and who you are. From this, you can be secure and even proud of yourself. From this, no lies need to be told.

Fading Out

There is this humongous thrift store just north of Chinatown here in L.A. I've been sticking my nose in there for the past twenty-five years or so. You never know what you will find...

Like most thrift stores it is hit-and-miss. Sometimes they have truly unique pieces of cultural memorabilia. Much of the time, they do not.

In any case, I had just started going through the vinyl. Somebody had obviously recently dumped their record collection and I was discovering a few truly unique pieces. Up walks this guy with a shopping cart. *"How much are the records,"* he asks. *"A dollar,"* I answer.

With this he begins to grab entire rows of LPs and put them in his cart. Since he started the conversation, I thought I would ask. *"Don't you care about the condition?"* *"No, it's not for anything like that."*

A prop guy. Obviously buying them for a set. I knew it the moment I saw him. Arms full of colorful newly applied ink, black jeans, and a tee-shirt.

Except for the row I was looking at. He grabbed pretty much every other piece of vinyl the store had to offer. I was a bit bummed. I mean, though I had just started, I was finding some good music. Now, it was gone. Gone forever...

What was going to happen to this music? It was obviously going to be used to decorate the set of some T.V. or film production, and then tossed in the trash. Lost to the hands of time...

Ever since the dawning of the age of CDs, I have realized that a lot of great music was going to be lost. Though I was one of the first to embrace this era – seeking out the first CDs you could find in record stores, I also knew with the coming of this new age, a lot of music was going to disappear.

There was so much great music, recorded on tape and released only on vinyl, that no one cared enough about to transfer it to the digital realm – first to CDs, then to MP3, and on to whatever comes next. Though it was great music there wasn't enough of a lasting audience for it to make the transition.

So these records, that music, like many, if not most, things in life, it will fade away into never-never-land – guided there by hands of a prop guy who doesn't care what condition the vinyl or the record sleeves are in. Sad…

Sometimes You See Strange Things

I was at *Starbucks* this morning. I was sitting outside on their patio. It was a cool, cloudy, L.A. day. An Asian woman walks past me. She was in her fifties or so.

She was Asian-American. I could tell this by the way she walked. She kind of dragged her feet along, as opposed to taking defined steps. And, her feet weren't completely in her shoes. Her heal was stepping on the back part of them. This is a very common pattern in parts of East Asia.

In any case, she walked past me and entered the garbage facility next to the patio section of this *Starbucks*. The unit that houses the large garbage bins for the entire complex is completely enclosed. So, once you are in, there is only one way out.

She entered, the doors closed behind her. I assumed that she was just going in to throw something away. But, she did not immediately reemerge.

I sat there. I finished my bagel. I finished my latte.' Still no reemergence of the lady.

I was done. So, I got up and left.

Why she was in there – what she was doing in there, I have no answer for you. Sometimes in life you just see strange things.

Scott Shaw Likes

For those of you who have wondered; I like:

French Cuff and/or Snap Shirts

Stetson Fedoras

Adidas Tennis Shoes
Though pretty much any tennis shoe with a vintage vibe will do...

New Balance 900 series tennis shoes
The last athletic shoes that are actually made in the U.S.A.

Gibson Guitars
I need a Gibson L5-S. I gave mine away when I was playing at the Montreal Jazz Festival a couple of years ago. If you feel like giving me one as a gift, that would be great!

Tokyo

The Rose Bowl Swap Meet

The PCC Flea Market

The Torrance Antique Street Fair

The Original Farmer's Market

Apple Computers

Modern Art

Music on Vinyl

Amoeba Music

KCRW

KXLU

The Vedanta Society Bookstore

Logos Bookstore

Green Apple Bookstore

Creative People

Positive People

Persian Cats

Freedom in the Hail

It hailed here in L.A. last night. I know you people who live in more intense climates than L.A. are saying, *"Whatever."* But, it is actually pretty rare for it to hail in L.A.

I remember the first time I experienced hail. I was maybe seven. By parents and I had just pulled up to our house in Southcentral L.A. My father had just recently purchased a new 1966 Mustang. It had been raining as we were driving home in the rain but when we got out of the car it had started to hail. *"What's this?" "That's hail."* I thought it was very cool. I stood outside and caught in my hand for a time.

Last night I was sitting around watching T.V. First it started to rain. Then I heard the pounding intensify on my roof. Hail, I knew it. Of course I had to go outside and experience it.

There are the two young brothers who live across the way from me. They are probably in the early and the last stages of high school. They both have long hair. I guess attempting to re-embrace an era gone by. In any case, I look over and they were out there on the street with no shirts on, running in the hail – collecting pieces of it and throwing it at each other.

It reminded me or my younger days when I would do things like tear my clothing off and jump in the freezing cold winter ocean in Big Sur. Or, when my Yosemite buddies and I would hike up to pools at lower Yosemite Falls on full moon nights, take our clothing off and dive in. The water was cold. You could only stay in there for a few moments. But, it was a true experience of emancipating freedom.

And, this is what makes life worth living. You must grab the moments of experience and freedom when you can. Last night, I stood in the hail.

Today, it is very clear and sunny in L.A.

Don't Let Your Eggs Get Cold

I was having breakfast at one of usual haunts. This guy walks in with his girlfriend. The host seats them at a table not far from mine. The guy was wearing one of those $100.00 plus ornamented tee shirts, a pair of those $300.00 jeans, and his hair was perfectly gelled. He was looking around to see if everyone was checking him out. I smiled to myself as I drank my coffee, awaiting my breakfast.

Immediately, he got on his phone and was talking very loudly about some business deal. The waitress came to take his order. He was very rude and very demanding.

As I've gone to this restaurant for a long time, I know many of the people who work there fairly well. The waitress looks over at me and rolls her eyes. I smile and shake my head.

With the order finally taken, the guy recommences with his ongoing and various phone conversations. He totally ignores his girlfriend who is simply staring off into space.

My food arrives. I began to eat it. Their food arrives and just as it does, the guy's phone rings again. He looks at the number and says to his girlfriend, in a very shady manner, I have to take this. He walks away from the table and goes to the outside of the restaurant to continue his conversation.

Never one to linger, I finish my breakfast and go to pay my bill. As I walk by their table, I notice that he ordered his eggs sunny side up.

Doesn't everybody hate cold eggs? But there they sat.

His girlfriend remained at the table eating her breakfast. I went and paid my bill. I left. The guy was outside, deeply engulfed in his conversation as his eggs got colder and colder.

The thing is, in life, you have set your perimeters. First of all, you have to be nice to people. No one likes an asshole. Second, when you are eating your breakfast, (or doing whatever it is you are doing), you should be doing that. That is simply the way to existence within a space of True Essence.

Be FULL in your moment. Do what you do. Don't let your eggs get cold.

The Powers That Be

I always find it interesting that so many of the things that affect our lives are completely out of our control. Yes, we have control over the small things: how we behave, how we treat other people, how we act or react. But, that is about it. Everything else can be altered by the actions of another and we have absolutely no control over it.

I mean, even at the most basic level of what we eat. Think how many times we have heard on the news that people have thought they were eating healthy food only to be poisoned by that food due to the vegetable being exposed to some toxin.

Me, I remember once I got really bad food poisoning from eating at this vegetation restaurant in Santa Barbara. Man, I thought I was going to die! And, a vegetarian restaurant is supposed to be clean and healthy!

But, those are just a couple of very obvious examples. I think we each have been hit by situations that affect our life and it simply dumbfounds us why it is happening to us, who is behind it, and/or what would be their motivation.

I received an email a couple of days ago. It was from a professor at a local college. She explained that she occasionally uses a book I wrote back in '89, *Cambodian Refugees in Long Beach, California,* as one of the books for her class. She goes on to tell me that she liked it so she wrote a positive review about it on Amazon. She says the review was up there for a couple of years. Then, it was gone. She thought there was some mistake so she put it back up and within a day it was gone again. She inquired, why? Amazon responded and told her that family members could not post reviews. She re-responded saying she was not a family member. They told her they will not reveal their, *"Research,"* but they know what they know.

Pretty funny, as I don't even know her and she is certainly not a family member. She doesn't even have the same family name or anything...

In any case, she contacted me, thinking I should know, and hoping I could do something about it.

I hadn't really looked at the book on Amazon for quite awhile. The last time I did there were several positive reviews. I looked. Now, they are all gone. The only one remaining is a very negative review.

Personally, I think all of this is very funny. Someone or something at the conglomerate of Amazon has a thorn in their paw about that book. Why? I have no idea. But, it just goes to show you, all this ridiculous stuff goes on that you have no control over but it affects your life. Most of the time, you do not even know that is going on, unless somebody brings your attention to it, like this lady did.

Is there anything I can do about it, as the professor hoped? Nope. What could I do?

So, I guess the moral of the story is, if you like something but the *Powers That Be* do not, they will attempt to alter the patterns of life and remove your positive review.

If you feel like it, you can try to put a positive one up there and see what happens. Maybe they won't consider you a family member. I don't know?

This is life. So much of it is totally out of our control. Some people get really obsessed and that is why they close-down, limiting all life-interaction; hoping this will limit their vulnerability.

Maybe that works, I don't know. Me, I like to live life. It is so short a time…

But ultimately, I guess the *Powers That Be* are in control. We are not. Hopefully they won't control us too much.

I Don't Want to Do Anything

I was kicking around today and I bumped into this girl I have known for a couple of years. She works at this one shop that I go into every now and then.

"Hey, how's it going?" I ask.
"The same. I'm trapped," she answers.

This girl always amuses me as she is one of those people that just emulates this essence of end-of-the-world negativity all the time.

I ask, *"Why? What is it that you want to do?"* Thinking that if there is something specific she wants, maybe I can help her.

"That's just it. I don't want to do anything," was her response.

This kind of life-attitude always amazes me. People that do not want to do anything. I've known a few people like this.

Me, I'm so ON, that I don't even like to ever waste a moment, because there is so much that I hope to accomplish.

Remembering back to when I was making the film, *Guns of El Chupacabra,* this girl who I was very close to in Thailand made her way to the States. Which is no small accomplishment in itself. I think people here in the West don't realize how hard it is for the average person to leave their home country if they hail from places like Southeast Asia. In any case, she was staying with her friend just a few blocks away from our production office in North Hollywood. I went to visit her one evening and I was speaking with the friend she was staying with.

"What do you do," I ask.
"Nothing. I used to work but I really just like to stay at home."

Wow. Though I like being at home too. There is such a world out there to experience. So many things to do. It baffles me how people want to hide away.

Yeah, there's a lot of bullshit too. But, you can't find the good if you don't seek it out.

I don't know? To each their own. Stay home. Do nothing. I guess we all are who we are and want what we want.

Yet, here we are. This is life. Just as in the case of the aforementioned girl, it seems that a lot of us want to be doing something other than what we are doing, even if what we want to be doing is doing nothing.

What do you want to do? Are you doing it? If not, why not?

People Don't Want to Know the Truth

People don't want to know the truth. They want to believe what they want to believe.

People don't investigate the truth. They make up their mind and then follow a course that allows them to hold on to and not diminish their beliefs.

How many times have you heard a person say, *"I was wrong in my beliefs and I am sorry that I spread the falsehood."* How many times have you heard a person exclaim, *"Sorry, I believed the wrong thing and I did something to hurt you. How can I fix that?"* Probably not very many.

People don't do it. They enter a subject based on their programing, what they have been told to believe, their hope to impress someone with their beliefs, and the desired outcome based upon their beliefs. That's how it is. But, that does not make anyone's beliefs valid.

The joke comedian George Carlin used to tell, *"How many Catholics have gone to hell because they ate meat on Friday,"* provides a good view into belief. For those of you who may not know, it was a Catholic tradition to not eat red meat on Fridays. In fact, it was considered a sin. Then, that tradition was overturned.

If traditions can be overturned by something as established as the Catholic Church, what does that say about your personal beliefs about a subject, a person, a religion, a politician, a war, a sporting event, a whatever?

Do you want to know the truth or do you want to believe based in your perceived reality? If you truly want to know the truth you must let go of your beliefs.

Snitch

When I was young one of the places I lived was in the section of Los Angeles that later became known as Koreatown. I was in junior high school during that period of my life. At this point in time the Los Angeles School District had instigated what they called, *"Busing."* What this meant was that they, *"Bused,"* children from lower-income communities to other sections of the city in order to increase segregation. For example, kids from South L.A., (Southcentral), were bused to the school I was attending.

This mandate eventually failed, as there was very little cultural interaction. The kids from South L.A. hung with the kids from South L.A. and the kids from the central city hung with their own.

Having spent a good portion of my youth in South L.A., this was a little different for me. There was certainly a part of my inner-makeup that related much more with the African-American kids than those who inhabited the neighborhoods around the school I was attending. But, that's a different story...

In any case, I used to speak with this one kid who was bused to the school. We had a few classes together. I wouldn't call him a friend, but we knew each other.

This kid always came off as very hard. He claimed gang affiliation and he often spoke of this fact. He stated he partied hard; i.e. taking drugs and drinking. I simply assumed he was who he claimed to be.

Back in the 1970s drugs were a counterculture way of life. And, I was certainly a willing member of that counterculture. Today, it has become very politically incorrect to be affiliated with drugs on any level. But, it was a different era back then. We were part of something. And, I make no apologies for my indulgences. In fact, I was a proud participant. Though I suppose I should state, it has been many-many years since I have indulged.

In any case, I had another crew of students who actually were my friends – those of us who were part of the counterculture; you know long hair, bell-bottom jeans, army jackets, and the like. One day, five or six of us were sitting out on the bleachers near the asphalt yard where the gym classes were held. This one girl, who actually had only a couple of fingers, was with us. I never asked what happed to her hands, but she was very well verse with using various utensils to get her business done with the few finger fingers she had remaining. In any case, she had gotten some weed from her parents and she was rolling us a joint. The aforementioned guy from South L.A. walks by and notices what we were doing. He immediately went and snitched on us. Here comes the coach!

Now, I guess I should launch a sidebar here… The coach was African-American and I had previously seen the kid cozying up to him. Maybe he had father issues; maybe he was looking for a father figure. I don't know? What I do know is that he alerted the coach to what we were doing.

The male coach grabbed my friend and myself, as we were the two males in attendance and took us to his office. The female coach came and led the three or four girls involved to her office.

We get inside his office, *"Empty your pocket! You better not be passing no pills at my school,"* exclaims the coach. *"Passing pills."* I smiled. None of us ever sold anything. If we had something and any of our friends wanted some, we would just give it to them.

Anyway, my friend and I emptied our pockets. We had no drugs. I actually had a roach clip that was shaped like a bullet. But, it just looked like a bullet. You had to take the top off to reveal the roach clip. I set it on the desk with my keys and my money. The coach found nothing. We were sternly dismissed.

But sadly, as the girl was actually the only person in possession of the weed, the police came and took her off to jail. I saw her handcuffed being escorted off of the campus. She was then expelled and she never returned to the school.

Today, the small amount of pot she had would probably have only equaled a ticket. But, back then, that was the Devil's Weed and people used to go down hard for even possessing a small amount. Stupid…

Anyway, I guess the moral of this story is, this is one of the first times that I realized that there are so many people out there who wish to present an image, like the guy who snitched on us. They want to come off as hard. They want to come off a gangsta.' They want to come off as whatever it is that they want to pretend they are. But, at their essence, people are never who or what they present themselves to be. Each person is a concoction that they have dreamed up.

And, who is to know? You never know until you know what is the actual truth about a person.

In most cases, you can never trust anyone. Because most people will sell you out at a moment's notices to either save their own ass or to cause themselves to rise up the ladder to whatever...

I've know people that one minute were telling me that soon they would be coming into a lot of money. Then, all of their friends were arrested, doing hard time, and all the person could do was to deny that he had anything to do with their incarceration – even though everyone knew this was not the case. He got caught first. He sold them out. And, these were his close friends.

People are not who they say they are. Be careful.

Dysfunctional Insanity

I was checking out the vinyl at a thrift store over on Santa Monica Blvd. in West Hollywood today and I start to hear a sound. It was a guy repeating a mantra, *"Ma Ra Sa, The Governor of the State of Montana. Ma Ra Sa, The Governor of the State of Montana. Ma Ra Sa, The Governor of the State of Montana."* He kept getting closer and then moving away from me. It was like a yoyo. Finally, he moved up very close to my back invading my personal space. I turned and looked at him. I smiled. He walked away. He stopped chanting.

The guy was nuts but I had to laughed to myself. Was the mantra he was chanting any less holy than those chanted for thousands of years in monasteries? Yes, yes, I know… Those mantras are supposed to invoke the divine via their sounds and their sound patterns. But, maybe to this guy, the Governor of Montana is holy. Who knows?

There is this guy who walks around the South Bay area of L.A., where I live. He wears dirty white pants and a dirty white tee shirt. He usually carries a Big Gulp. The guy must walk for miles upon miles everyday as I have seen him for years all over the South Bay. Generally, he is screaming some bit of insanity at the top of his lungs. A few weeks ago I pull up to a stoplight and there he was. He walks up to the cross walk deep in his rambles. He waits for the light to turn green. He becomes silent. He walks across the street right in front of me saying nothing. He gets to the other side. Again, he recommences his ranting and raving of, *"Shit, fuck,"* at whomever or whatever he is screaming at. Whenever I have seen him I have wondered, what does he do at night when he is not howling in the sunlight?

But, at least with all his walking, he stays in shape.

I was walking down the street with my lady a few years ago in Berkeley. There was this guy on the street rambling all kinds of nonsense to no one's ears but his own. He was shit-nuts. As I came close to him, he stopped. He very calmly inquires of me, *"How's it going?"* *"Everything is fine,"* I reply. I walk on. As soon as I get some distance, his insane ramblings recommence.

As the truth, which has become a joke among my close friends goes, *"Animals, kids, and crazy people all love me."* Why, I don't know. But, they all seem to.

I think we have all seen crazy people hanging out here or there as we have passed through life. Thank god we are not like that. But, think how many people are. Not their fault. Just their biology. And, it is only the not taking their medication for one day that sends them down the road to pure dysfunctional insanity.

This is life. Say, *"Hi,"* to it's inhabitants.

The Beachside Table

There is this beach city restaurant that I frequent. I've been going there for like thirty years. Recently I noticed that this one new customer had been showing up in the mornings. The only reason I noticed is that he would be there when I arrived, reading the newspaper, and still be there when I left.

The guy in question is maybe sixty. He always wears this messy *Members Only* jacket. For those of you who may not know, *Members Only* jackets were popular in the early 1980s. Now, they are predominately worn by older people refusing to let go of an era or by hipsters attempting to grab a time gone past. But, they're really ugly jackets.

Anyway, I hit the restaurant yesterday in the AM. The guy was there. He always sits at this one table – the one which is considered to have the best view. The funny thing is, he sits with his back to the wall. Looking away from the ocean. The reason I know he will only sit at this table is I have seen him arrive later than me and if I or someone else is at that table, he will wait outside, newspapers and backpack in hand, until it become available.

What a weird thing to be obsessed about.

Yesterday, I show up. I sit down. He had finished his breakfast, yet he sat there reading the paper. He instructed the waitress to get him a new, fresh cup of coffee. He was going to be there awhile.

He read. I ordered. I ate. I finished. He takes another part of the newspaper and begins to do the crossword puzzle. He wasn't going anywhere soon.

The reason I bring this up is that this is a popular restaurant. Space is at a premium. And, space, (the tables), is how the people that work there make their money. Yet, this guy sits there, at the best table in the house, for how long, I do not know – taking up the space and keeping the people that work there from making more money from other customers.

Some people are just so rude, so self-involved, so obsessive that they do not take the time to see the big picture and view or care about the affect they are having on others.

How do you operate your life? Do you think about others when you do what you do?

Art is Everywhere

This morning I wake up. The morning sun is shining in. It is passing through the bamboo bead door curtain that hangs outside of my bedroom. The sunlight is etching an image almost like a lens flare across the wall.

If you take a moment to look at and study your environment even the most common things become objects of pure beauty. They become art.

Art does not have to be a painting or a photograph. Art is everywhere. You simply have to open your eyes and see it.

The End of Days

I was listening to NPR last week and this guy was detailing how throughout the years many software developers had gone out of business leaving people who used their software with items they could no longer access. In his case, he was a music producer and, as he stated, he had tons of music reordered on floppy disks that could not be opened.

For any of us who have been using computers for a long time we have witness this process. Operating systems and programs have gone by the wayside.

I was there in the early days of the first personal computers and I can attest that many things have changed and much has been lost. In my case, I have always transferred the music I recorded via computers to other accessible media before the program went away or I moved on from the operating system. But, I have lost a lot of creations to computers, as well. A number of screenplays I have written, (yes, yes, I have written screenplays), are gone. Most notably is the one I wrote for, *The Roller Blade Seven*. The executive producer wanted to know what we were going to film, I was the one assigned to write it. I did, but I gave all my copies away. And, as is well know, *The Roller Blade Seven* became the first Zen Film, so that script wasn't used. Operating system changed. Disk unreadable. Gone forever...

But, more than just software going away, systems crash, floppies corrupt, and things get lost. An ideal example of this happened when I was writing, *Nirvana in a Nutshell*. This was back when Macs had very small memory capacity so I kept everything on a disk. I was done. The book was on a disk. I went to put it in the computer to print it out to send it to the publisher. But, the disk, for whatever reason, became corrupted. I spent a lot of money trying to get computer specialists to get the data from the disk but they could do nothing. Fuck me! I had to rewrite the whole book. The original one is lost to the Akashic Record forever...

But, more than just creations – times and life change; places changes, they go out of business. For example, there was the great restaurant in Santa Monica called, *Hamburger Henry's*. It was across the street from one the seminal Punk Rock clubs of Punk's heyday in L.A., *Madam Wong's West*. We used to play there, as did all of the essential Punk and New Wave bands of the era. We would go and get our food on before we would play or when we would go to watch other bands.

I don't miss the club, that went away as times changed. But, *Hamburger Henry's lasted* from the late 70s into the near-mid 90s. They had great food. I loved their Caviar Burger and French Onion Soup. Nothing has compared since.

Also in Santa Monica was the best Italian Restaurant ever, *Anna Maria's*. The owner, Anna Maria, would walk around singing Italian songs and talking to her guests. They loved me there. Great food. Great experience. But, by the early 90s it was gone.

Picking up the slack came this restaurant in Hermosa, *Rocky Cola*. This is the only place I knew where you could eat really healthy food made with brown rice or go for a Philly Cheesesteak sandwich. That lasted up until about a year ago. But now, it too is gone...

Those are just a couple of examples, but I guess that is the thing that lets you know you are getting old, when you can look back to the, what was, and compare it to the, what is, and know that something is missing – understand that something important, something great, is lost forever and others will never be able to experience it.

Painting on Paper

There is this shop in *Little Tokyo* here in L.A. It is owned and operated by this lady. It is very interesting to watch her open her shop. She has all kinds of stuff that she puts out in front. It probably takes her about twenty minutes to get everything arranged and rearranged to her contentment. It is very precise and methodical. She does this while people continually attempted to enter her doors. *"Not now. Come back in fifteen minutes,"* she says.

Inside the shop she has a large amount of John Lennon memorabilia. Much of it is not for sale. She even has a John Lennon VHS tape in its original box on one of her shelves. *"Not for sale,"* so it says.

Perhaps most interesting is the fact that she has a number of John Lennon lithographs hanging on her walls. They are definitely his artwork but were released after his passing. They are signed by Yoko Ono and they have her red Asian stamp of approval.

As there is a lot of sunlight coming into this ladies shop, if you look at these lithos you can see that many of them have become browned and in some cases Yoko's signature and stamp have faded. Time has taken its toll.

That's the thing about painting on paper. Or, in this case, doing a litho on paper. They don't last. Paper just does not have the resiliency of paint upon canvas. Canvas ages too. But, if you look at old canvas, particular at the back of the painting, you can see that though it has aged, the weaving of the threads can hold it together for centuries.

In some ways I think it is sad that after a person's passing people take their creations and make new, less original pieces with them, and then market them to the masses. But, in some cases, people buy them and put a sticker on them, *"Not for sale."* Then, just as is the case with life, they hold onto them as they fade into the abyss of the hands of time.

    How do you cast your creations to eternity?

Answers Verses Opinions

An answer is an absolute fact given in response to a question.

An opinion is what someone thinks about a subject given in response to a question.

We have each asked questions of others in our life. We may have wanted another person's guidance when we were making a decision or we may have been confused about which road to walk down so we ask what someone else thinks.

By asking someone something, you have opened up the door to allowing that person to guide your life course. The problem is, most people confuse what they feel, what they think, and what they believe with fact.

No doubt, each of us can look back to a point in our life when we received guidance from someone. Whether it was asked for or not, they gave it to us and we listened. But, once we took their advice we later realized that it was totally wrong and that it set an unwanted course of events in motion in our life. We realized that we should have not taken their advice and we should have gone in a different direction. This different direction may have included not buying a particular product, not taking part in a specific event, not going to this place or that, not getting involved in a certain relationship, and so on. But, we listened and the deed was done. There was no going back.

It is for this reason, that you should never confuse your opinion with fact. It is also for this reason that you should never veil your opinion as fact. Because once you answer a person's question and once they walk down the road you suggest, you are responsible for them taking that path. Their choice becomes your karma. And, from this, all the right or all the wrong rests on your shoulders.

2nd

I was kicking around Guitar Center.com about a week ago and I noticed that one of their stores in Minnesota was offering a 1982 *Yamaha FG-512* 12-String for sale. I was looking for another 12-String and I was happy to see this one being offered.

I actually bought one of these guitars new back in '82. What I did with it, I don't remember – sold it, gave it away; I don't know? A lot of guitars have passed through my hands over the years. But, I do remember buying it very clearly. I had picked it up at a guitar shop on Santa Monica Blvd. in Hollywood, named, *Guitar Villa*.

Thought I have always been primarily a Guild man, (it terms of acoustics), at least until Fender bought the company and then began making a lot of their product in China. In any case, the reason I originally liked this Yamaha so much was that it had this very bright, distinctive sound.

Though I am not a fan of buying vintage guitars online, because you are never really quite sure of what you will end up with, I decided to go for it.

Today it arrived. I opened the box. The first thing I checked for, as I took it out of the box, was the neck. Yamaha's of that era were known for having their necks bow over time. Looked good. I was happy. But then, as I pulled it farther out of the box, I realized that it had some cracks in its back. I looked closer, perfectly repaired but... Then I noticed its label. It was red stamped, "2nd." My first though was that is pretty messed up of Guitar Center not to mention this fact, as it impacts the value of a guitar immensely.

I studied the guitar closely and the perfectly repaired cracks in the back were most probably the cause of the, "2nd." I was upset.

I called Guitar Center Customer Service center to set up a return. The guy asked me, *"But, how does the guitar sound?"* That question annoyed me a little bit. *"How should I know! It has repaired cracks in its back! Why would I even try to play it,"* I exclaimed.

The Customer Service guy apologized for the store not mentioning this in their on-line ad. *"It's not your fault,"* I responded. He told me I could take it back to my local Guitar Center for a refund.

After the phone call, I studied the guitar a bit farther. I decided to tune it up and give it a go. Yes, it did have the distinctive tone of the one I owned many years ago, though it did need a new set of stings.

So, here is the question of life. Yes, it is a 2nd. Yes, it has been broken and then repaired. Yes, its value is greatly diminished. But, can what it has to offer be of use to me? Can it be a part of my creative process? Or, will I only be able to focus on its flaws?

How many things in life have been broken than fixed? How many people have been hurt, injured, used, broken, and then they must try to get on with their life? If we don't give these things/these people the opportunity to be of use, then what will all this creation equal?

Do things only have to be perfect and pristine to be appreciated?

Everything Used To Be On Wheels

In the latter part of the 1980s and into the 1990s a lot of the furniture was created on wheels. Computer desks, coffee tables, dinning room tables, couches, bookshelves, and all the etcetera used to be created upon a wheel-based design. It was great, when you wanted to move things around it was very easy.

Stores like *Ikea, Z Gallery,* and even *Staples* had a bunch of really usable furniture based on wheels. Now, it is all gone. I was recently looking for a new desk and I went to all the above listed places and more, but nothing. Nothing is created on wheels anymore.

Back in the day I had several items, most notable a few computer desks, which were on wheels. By my nature, I am not a nostalgic person. When I need something new, I move on, and let go of the old. So, I gave away all of my previous on-wheel desks. My loss, I guess. Because I can no longer find any desks created in this manner.

Hold on and become a hoarder or let go and need what you once had. An interesting life question…

Remember When It Was So Important To Watch Music Videos?

I was sitting around flipping channels last night. There was nothing really worth watching. Of the hundreds of channels I have, nothing... *"Pretty amazing,"* I thought. I popped over to one of MTVs remaining music channels. There was a good song playing by an obscure band that I heard on KCRW. I didn't know the name of the band, but it caused me to stop and watch. The video was okay. Not great. Just okay...

I looked over to my lady and realized/asked, *"Remember when it was so important to watch music videos?" "Oh yeah,"* she responded. She continued by naming the list of shows here in L.A. that actually used to play music videos at various times of the day and night in the early 1980s. There was this one show on at three in the afternoon, one on at midnight on Friday, and the etcetera. I smiled. That was a long time ago.

When MTV came around a bit after this, it really changed everything. (I know... I know... I'm dating myself here.) But, back then, it was really important to watch music videos and watch for new music videos. It really felt like an accomplishment.

I remember back in my twenties when MTV broke through. I was living in Hermosa Beach and I had this big kitchen that I used to staple canvases to the wall and paint. I'd have the coffee pot going and MTV on. If a new video came on, I would run in and tape it on my video deck. I never really rewatched them. But, it was just a feeling that you had to catch that moment.

Really... A lot of revolutionary filmmaking was being unleashed in the genre of music videos at that time in history. But now, that has all changed. The funny thing is, in many cases, I will hear a song I like on the radio or something but then when I see the music video, (if I ever do), I will wish that I did not know what that person or that band looked like; as they're just not very appealing and the video isn't very good.

And also, and probably more importantly, the craft and the art of pushing the boundaries of filmmaking seems to be gone in music videos. It has just become rehashed versions of people posing for the camera. Nothing revolutionary in that...

I don't know... Watching music videos every now and then is something to do. But, it certainly no longer seem very important or educational.

Nobody Wants to See Old People Dance

I'm remembering back to when I truly came upon the realization that nobody wants to see old people dance. I was going to a club in downtown L.A. a little over twenty years ago and just in front of me, entering the club, was this L.A. newscaster. He was on a station here in L.A. during the primetime hours. He was a very conservative looking guy with red hair. With him was his wife, wearing a very wifely flora dress.

Obviously, the girl I was with and I took notice of them. It just seemed kind of strange seeing this guy going into a nightclub with pounding dance music.

In any case, we got a table, had a drink or two, and then hit out to the dance floor. As we moved, I looked over and there he and his wife were, stiffly dancing away.

It was not that he and his wife were so old. They were probably forty or so. And, I am sure they were having fun. It was just the vibe and the attitude they encompassed… It was not young, free, rhythmic, or anything like that. It was like they shouldn't be there. They needed to be somewhere else, doing something else. From that scene I understood that there would come a point when I would stop dancing.

I have always kept that image in mind. It is one of those things that each of us, as we get older, must be willing to do. We must be wiling to let the things of youth go or we just look stupid. Though I always loved to dance, I no longer force others to witness it. :-)

I believe we can each think back to when we were young. When you were ten, twenty was so old.

When you were twenty, thirty was so old. And, forty or fifty, forget about it... That was ancient.

Personally, I have always enjoyed the process of aging. It has never bothered me to get older and to tell people my true age. I'm proud and amazed at it. The fact is, I never thought I would make it this long or this far. But, I did.

That being said, I had a discussion a few years back with a friend of mine that I had met in San Francisco back in the 70s. She is my age. We were speaking about this subject and she exclaimed, *"I will never stop dancing."* I smiled. *"Good for her,"* I thought. But, that being said, I must stick to the main premise. If we live long enough, we all get old and with that we must not burden the youth, in a youthful environment, with seeing our age unveiled.

A funny side note here is, maybe a year or so before I had my realization, a friend of my and I were doing our usual Tuesday night at this one nightclub in West Hollywood we hit each week. Each Tuesday there would be this old guy, and I mean old: deep fifties, maybe sixties. He would be out there in the middle of the dance floor flaying his arms and moving his feet to the heavy metal music that blasted through the speakers. My friend joking said, *"That'll be us some day..."*

Well no, not me anyway... You've got to leave the youthful things to the young.

Where You Plant Your Seeds

When I was growing up I was obviously drawn to the Spiritual Path. The Eastern side of metaphysics was my primary focus. That being said, it was a time in the spiritual history of the U.S., and the world for that matter, when everyone and every spiritual group were very accepting of each other. Times have changed. Now, it is all about, "I am this and you are that." Not good, I think. But, that is just the way it is. In time, that mindset may all change again.

In any case, there was a spiritual brotherhood that was in existence when I was in my teens and into my early twenties. They were known as, *The Blanket Brothers*. They were Christian *sadhus*. They had no home and roamed around the West Coast wearing only a tunic, Jesus-like garment. They did not cut their hair or shave. They wore no shoes, had no possessions, and lived a very humble life; owning only a blanket. Their purpose was to pray and become in tune with the spiritual essence of Jesus.

Every now and then you would see a *Blanket Brother* walking down the Sunset Strip, on Hollywood Blvd, or in Venice. They truly embodied the spiritual essence of, *The Essenes*.

Just as this was a time when the various spiritual traditions were very interactive, it was also a time when there was a lot of respect given to those who lived the path of asceticism. You would see a *Blanket Brother* and understand that they were a person who was truly attempting to interact with true spiritual essence and leave behind the ways of the world.

Again, times have changed. Now they would just be seen as a bum.

Today, if you search for the *Blanket Brothers* on the Internet it would difficult to find anything. Somewhere along the way, in these changing times, *the Blanket Brothers* were gone. Gone but not forgotten. Their sect may have disintegrated into the abyss of a world that shifted from spirituality to selfishness, but what they lived did aid in the overall growth of consciousness that helped to frame and define a generation.

It is from the actions of people like *the Blanket Brothers* that ancient spiritual traditions thrive through the ages. It is also through the actions of people like *the Blanket Brothers* that they allowed people to understand, even if only for a moment, that there is more to life then simply seeking personal gain.

Belief

If Christmas is always on the same day, why does the date of Eastern change every year? Well, there are a few very simple reasons for this. The ancient Christian Church fathers wanted to have Eastern near the Jewish Passover and the whole Solar/Lunar Calendar thing…

Anyway… We have just moved through the Eastern season. Whenever there is a substantial Christian holiday, like Easter, there are a lot of good documentaries about the Bible, its evolution, the history of Christianity, and Jesus that they play on the various channels. It is really a time when you can learn a lot by simply watching T.V.

Though I was born into a Christian family, and was indoctrinated into Christianity through Church and Sunday School; I am not a Christian. That being said, I have always found the evolution of Christianity very interesting and have studied it in-depth. I did this way back when you actually had to find books and read about the subject before there were all these great documentaries on the subject that played on T.V.

Christianity is a very interesting faith. A lot of people believe. But, the thing about belief is that most people do not know why they believe. They simply do. This is where the various religions and religious sects get their members. They get them by belief, not by proof. And, the difference between belief and proof is vast.

As I have study the evolution of Christianity to a substantial degree there has been times when I have gotten into discussions with Christians about the way the religion evolved, what is and is not known, and how books like the bible actually came into existences. In some cases, the people I was discussing the issue with became very mad at me, *"You're going to hell,"* and all that stuff. In other cases, the discussion simply ended with, *"It's all about faith. It is all about believing."*

Perhaps that is the best way to define life. We each believe what we believe. Some of us search through all the rhetoric and attempt to emerge with a firm grasp of the subject. Others of us simply want to believe and never question the how or the why. I don't know that either one is better. I only know what is right for me. But, at the end of the day, our belief, in whatever we believe in, is all we have.

A funny side note in closing… When I was about thirteen I was already deeply involved in Eastern Metaphysics but I decided that maybe I should re-explore my Christian roots. So, a friend of mine and I went into a church over on 3rd Street here L.A. That was when I was living in the section of the city that later became known as Koreatown. We were quietly sitting there pondering reality. Soon after we arrived the minister came up to us and told us we had to leave. He did this after looking us up and down. I guess he didn't like our long hair. That was back when long hair on a man was taboo. Didn't Jesus have long hair? Anyway, we got up and left. So much for me getting back into Christianity. I was shunned away by a minister. :-)

Somebody Told Me

Somebody told you something about another person. Of course, you believed them. Why would they lie? You based your entire appraisal of the person by what somebody else had told you about them. Once you were told, you spread the knowledge forward and you told other people what the original person had told you. Much later you found out none of it was true.

It is human nature that we believe what people say. We believe them, until we have a reason not to believe them. We believe other people because we want to believe other people. But, what always must be taken into consideration is that each person has their own agenda, their own motivations. When they speak about anyone or anything they are doing so from their own perspective and they present information about anyone or anything, to other people, for a very specific reason.

Why does anybody talk about anybody or anything at all? They do so because they want to propagate knowledge from a very specific point of view.

I knew this one person that loved to stir things up. He was always going around saying that a person said this or that. He caused so many people to dislike one another and even, in some cases, enter into confrontations. The thing was, what he told people about other people was rarely based upon fact. It was at best a distorted partial truth and most probably a flat-out lie. Yet, he went through his entire life like this. He talked, people listened.

A lot of people lost their friendships due to this man and, in fact, lost the chance for the further evolution of their life due to their dissociation from people who could have actually helped them move forward. All this based upon what one man told them.

Most cases are not that exaggerated. But, each person is motived by their own set of psychological parameters and desires for an end result. If someone loves somebody they say only the most glowing things. If, on the other hand, somebody dislikes someone or wants to guides people's opinions about that person in a negative direction, they discuss demeaning things about that person. As was the case of the previously described individual, they may even misquote a person and say things that they did not say simply to get an emotional rise out of another person.

The ultimate understanding of human interaction is, you should only believe what you know to be true. Never based your judgment upon what someone said about someone or something.

Truth is easily observed. Words mean nothing.

The Lab

I was kickin' around *The Lab* yesterday. For those of you who may not know, *The Lab* is this shopping plaza in Orange County that has been around since the 80s that has some interesting shops. They bill it as, *"The Anti Mall."*

I had picked up a few pieces of vinyl at this little record store that is located in and around an old Airstream trailer and afterwords I was walking around and I noticed this couple from Japan. They were in their late thirties-early forties. The guy had very long hair on one side of his head and a crew cut on the other. This is a hairstyle that a few people rocked back in the early 1980s. The girl I was with joking commented, *"He has a partying going on one side of his brain and is all business on the other."*

The next group I noticed was made up a very tall African-American girl who added to her height with very-very large platform shoes and some very extreme sunglasses. She was flanked by a girl with corpse makeup on her face. You know the kind of makeup, it made her look like she was dead. This was a look worn by people who were into the Death Rock movement back in the 80s, long before it became known as Goth. I wondered if she listened to bands like *45 Grave.*

As I have long said, so few people hold on to any sense of style as they enter into adulthood. Everybody just blends in with the masses. And, I think this is very sad.

Though the people I saw were basically emulating styles from a different era, they each did a great job of bringing it into the now and expressing something other than the every-day.

I have passed though a few periods of life when style was at the forefront and people truly represented who they were. The 60s into the 70s had the hippie culture. The 70s into the 80s had the punk, new wave culture. Each of these eras truly breathed new levels of style and expression into society. But, like most people lose any sense of unique style and self-expression as they grow into adulthood, so too did these eras fade. Hopefully a new era, filled with style, will emerge in the near future.

But ultimately, it was just nice to be reminded that some people still step up and express whom they are. They do not choose to blend into the masses. They want to be something more, representing something different than the boring mainstream, seen-it-all-before, culture.

Do You Think About Others Before You Do What You Do?

I was driving in Hermosa Beach this morning. I was on this one street where you veer off to the left and it feeds into another street. There is a slight hill and a stop sign just before you make your final turn onto the new street. In front of me was a Volvo SUV. It stopped at the stop sign but then did not move forward. I was in a patient mood so I sat there for a few moments. A car pulled up behind me and honked its horn. The Volvo sat for a few more moments and then proceeded forward. Immediately, it turned to the left and went into a garage.

Though I did not realize it initially, because I could not see around the SUV, what the driver was doing was that he had pushed his garage door opener and was waiting for the garage to open. The driver sat there at the stop sign not caring about what affect he had on the flow of traffic. He was content to wait until he could drive straight into his garage.

Do you think about others before you do what you do? Most people do not. This is the primary cause of all the problems in the world. People only think about themselves.

When things are going well in life most people proceed down their merry path and couldn't care less what negative effect they are having on others. They're happy, and who cares about anyone else. But, when things start to go wrong in their life, they become very upset – they become the victim and seek solace wherever they can find it. *"Look at me, my life is so bad..."* But, they never look to themselves to see what their previous actions have set in motion.

It does not matter if what you are doing in a specific moment does not negatively affect you. If it negatively affects others, there is a problem. And further problems will be set in motion by the initial problem you created.

I cannot emphasize enough that you must always be very aware of how what you are doing is affecting others. If you care about people, if you care about humanity, if you care about this world, you must consider others before you do anything that may negatively impact people or this planet. If you want to stop the negatively, it must begin with you.

Make this Life-Place a better Place.

People Fall Away

I have always found it interesting how people come and go in our lives. In some cases, they piss us off or we piss them off and that is the motivation to move along. Sometimes people get married; have kids, and that is the cause to grow apart. As you get older, there are also the people who pass away – move onto the next world. As time goes by, that sadly happens more and more frequently to the people you know. There's no stopping the cruel hands of time... And, in other cases, people simply move to other cities, other places, and you lose touch. But, then there are the other situations. The situations where you are truly close to a person and, for some unexplained reason, you simply drift apart. When you look back you wonder why.

For me, there have been a few examples that seem to illustrate the later of these situations quite well. For example, there was my one friend. We were best buds in high school; traveled up and down the West Coast between San Diego and into Canada; we drank a lot, played music together, slam danced when punk was new, (before slam dancing became moshing), and had a lot of years of fun. He even got married, had a kid, and raised a couple of others. But, every Saturday I was invited over. We would work on his house, drink beer all day, and then sit down to have dinner each Saturday evening. They were the family I never really had. After dinner we'd watch some T.V., then he'd drift off into family life and I would hit out to the gothic underworld of L.A. Or, if we were too drunk his wife would get me a pillow and a blanket and I would sleep on what had become known as, *"My home away from home,"* their couch. Time went on, I got into the film game, his wife passed away, and we each moved forward into our own realms of reality. I never see him anymore. Why? I don't really know...

I had another friend who I met in high school. By then I was already deeply involved in eastern mysticism and that is what drew us together. He was a couple of years older than I and he graduate. That was back when high school was just three grades: tenth through twelfth, at least here in L.A. Anyway, I had not seen him for a long time but one night, when I was a junior in high school, there was a knock on the door of my apartment in Hollywood. There he was. For the next few years we explored the various realms of eastern spirituality together, traveled up and down the coast, went to a lot of great punk shows – before punk rock was punk rock, and were very good friends. He eventually moved to Santa Cruz with his college roommate to transfer from CSUN to UC Santa Cruz. I help them load their moving van and actually drove the U-Haul up the coast for them in the middle of the night. It was pretty scary. I was only seventeen.

I would go and visit him in Santa Cruz, but eventually we lost touch. A few years later, after I had returned from India and was in graduate school, I was in Santa Cruz with my girlfriend and one evening we went into a record shop and there he was behind the counter. It was so strange... We spoke for a few moments but I didn't even know what to say to him. I never saw him again... But, I do remember our friendship.

Another friend was this guy I met at the Sufi Dances, (The Dances of Universal Peace). I actually met a lot of people there. I was still in Hollywood High School and he had graduated the year before from a different school. We became very close. We hung out a lot. We traveled to spiritual centers up and down the coast, chanted to our hearts content, and hung in the various spiritual locations around the area. He too eventually moved to Santa Cruz to attend college. Santa Cruz was the spiritual hub of the universe at that point in history. I would visit him, stay in my van out in front of his house. He would come down and visit me. But, somewhere, for some reason, we lost touch. I guess that's life. Some people we hold onto no matter what. Some people hold on to us no matter what. In other cases, we just stop communication and there is no real reason why.

These situations are a very good example of life. In the end, we all pass into the abyss. Those who pass before us, we remember. Those who are still here when we move along, hopefully they will remember us. In the end it is all gone.

Welcome to life.

Process Verse Product

On the Spiritual Path, *"The Process,"* is forever touted as being the true goal. The getting there is every bit as important as the arriving. Maybe...

From my personal perspective, I prefer the getting it done – being there and then looking back. But, that's just me.

Particularly in the Japanese Zen Culture they have devised all kinds of techniques to make, *"The Getting There,"* a meditation. For example, meditative walking: taking one-step, bowing, and then continuing, the Tea Ceremony that takes forever and ever. And, so on.

But, to me this all seems like Mind Games – pretending you are doing something instead of actually doing it. Sure, all of that STUFF does make it more of an experience but it also wastes a lot of Life-Time. To me it is simply pretending. Because if you're not there, you're not there. If you have not arrived, have not finished, then you have no True-Knowledge of the whole experience, only expectations of what you believe will occur.

In terms of Real-Life I have known a lot of people who are very painstaking at all that they do, especially in the arts. If they write a book or a screenplay they contemplate every word before it is every placed on paper or on the computer screen. That's fine, if that's how you want to do it, but it has not made them any more successful at their craft. Me, when I write, I write. A screenplay, I write in a day or two. A novel, the same. I believe; if it is already in your brain, get it out! You don't need to over think it. You simply need to do it.

Just like with film editing, most editors plan to complete three to five minutes a day of finished footage. That's stupid and insane. It's a waste of time and simply a way to get a bigger paycheck. I have always been able to work super fast as a film editor. An example is *Armageddon Blvd.* I edited the whole film in two days.

But, I guess there are a few exceptions, more geared towards the world of the mundane. For example, is you like coffee an old-school percolator is so much cooler and better tasting than a modern coffee maker. Sure you can set the timer on a coffee maker and it will be ready when you wake up but just the process of percolating coffee just makes the doing worth the doing.

I guess that's the choice of life: *Doing Worth Doing or Doing Worth Not Doing*

Your life. Your choice.

Your Past Haunts You

"That will go down on your permanent record." That was always the vague threat that has been given to people. But, except for a criminal record and maybe something the government has, there is no, *"Permeate Record."* That being said, you are defined by your past. What you have done can and probably will come back to haunt you. It is for this reason that everything you do needs to be done with an intended purpose or it can alter the future you hope for yourself.

In my case, I have walked a spiritual path over to one side of the spectrum that was not defined by commonality. I forever detail my own experiences because I do not want there to be any confusion about who or what I am and what I have or have not done. Most people are not like this, however. They may do what they do but then when what they have done no longer suits their image of themselves they attempt to hide it.

You know there is all kinds of things people do. They may steal, hurt people, take drugs, have multiple, illicit sexual relationships, have an affair, and the all and the everything of what you can think of. When they are doing these activities, they probably know it is not good and/or wrong but they do it anyway, for whatever reason.

This is where life gets messy. People know what they are doing is not good. Though it may feel good, they know it is not good. Not good in terms of the future. But, once it is done, it is done, and that is that. What you have done is cast to the realms of forever. And, no matter how hard you may try to hide what you have done, (or hide from it), there is the potential that it will come back and haunt you.

So, first of all, if you are afraid of the implications, if you know what you are about to do is not right, don't do it. But, if you have already done it, then what? If your past has come back to haunt you, what can you do? If your relationships or your health is damaged by your past actions, what can be done? Really, there is nothing that you can do. You can't undo what you have done. And, hiding from it only drives it deeper into the realms of what you hope will not be found out.

So, own it. Own what you were, who you are, and what you hope to be. With this, the veil of illusion is lifted and you can, at least, move forward not solely defined by hiding who you were but experiencing what you are to become.

Creation and Adaptation

You will forever be defined by what is available to you. This is particularly the case in terms of creativity.

If you don't have a paintbrush, you can't paint. But, that does not mean you cannot do something else.

In all aspects of creativity there are things that you may want to create. The reality of creativity is, however, you can only work within the realms of what you have available to you. This goes to all levels of creation.

For example, if you want to paint you will need a canvas, paints, and paintbrushes. These items are pretty easy to come by and are relatively inexpensive. Once you have acquired those basic elements you can move forward. But, what if you desire to use the color blue in your painting and you do not have it? It is at this point that many people will stop, (or never start), the painting and dream of the day when they will have some blue paint.

This is obviously an analogy but this is what most people do and why they never succeed in being the creative person they hope to become. They stop before they ever begin.

The other way to handle this situation is to use whatever color you have on hand and move foreword with your painting. By employing this method you get your painting competed.

As an artist, I say all the time, if you have expectations your painting will never turn out exactly the way you expected it to. This is the case even if you spend day-upon-day, month-upon-month, work and re-work it – the painting will still ultimately come out different from what you anticipate.

This is good. This is what True Art is – letting the Art be the end-all of what you create – not simply your domination over the canvas. By allowing yourself to accept the art as it presents itself, it is free, it is True Art. But, this not the way most people come at art.

A personal example here is, I recently bought a large quantity of acrylic paint from this art supply warehouse in Orange County. Normally, I like to start and finishing a painting in one sitting. But, this paint is a little watery. So, I have no choice. First I have lay-down the backdrop of the painting, let it dry, then return and paint the central subject matter later. That's not ideal for me, but it is what I must do if I want to use the paint and create the painting.

Being dominated by external circumstances and situations goes much further than simply paint upon canvas. When you go into the more complex realms of art, such as the creation of music and cinema, things get even more complicated. Sure, a guy can go and play his acoustic guitar anywhere. Sure, an actor can go and actor anyplace. But, if you want to capture these creations for eternity than you must deal with technology. And, as I have long stated, *"In a mechanical world there are mechanical problems."*

It is a simple fact of creative life, you probably are not going to have all the technology that you want at your disposal and you probably will run into some problems along your path to creation using technology. You can let that stop you, as it has many would-be creators, or you can move past your limitations and get something done.

As a filmmaker, pretty much since I began, I have run into limitations of what I have had available to me in the process of film creation. Mostly, this has been dominated by money, or the lack thereof. I mean, we can look to people like Francis Ford Coppola when he was making, *Apocalypse Now.* The stories have long been told how he would do take after take of the same scene which cause all kinds of cast and crew problems and forced the film to go insanely over budget. Or, Michael Cimino's, *Heaven's Gate,* which followed a similar path of creative obsession. Great movies, but most filmmakers do not have the ability to take filmmaking to that level of obsession. Again, this is why most would-be filmmakers may have an idea but never get it completed because they refuse to understand when enough is enough and that you have to live with what you have if you actually want to complete a film.

As an indie filmmaker for more than twenty years I can say with authority if you want to get your film made you need to do it with what is available. If you do not want to be one of those people who simply talks about making a film forever, you have to make your movie with what you can get a hold of and then, more importantly, you need to accept and appreciate the finish product for what it is. It is probably not going to be Apocalypse Now but it will be a film that you have competed.

You can obsess if you want. But, if you desire to get anything completed, you have to be willing to accept. You have to let it be what it is. For example, one of the first films I produced was The Roller Blade Seven. Don Jackson and I took the film's edited footage with time code to an online editing facility to have it constructed for final output. We spent quite a lot of time there, days-upon-days. In one scene we had Don Stroud's character continuing to laugh off-screen as the lead actress skated off into the desert. It was really very dramatic. But, when we sat down for the final watch, the laugh track was gone. The online editor looked at us. He knew he had blown it. The problem was, going back and putting it in would have been very-very time consuming and expensive. Though it was the online editors fault and we could have pushed the issue, we did not. We had a delivery date, so we let it go. Not ideal, but it was the choice that we had to make.

That is the ultimate point of all this. You can choose to create; you can decided to be a creator, and move forward with whatever limitations you possess in order to get your vision out there. Or, you can sit back, waste your life, and always be the person saying, *"I am going to do that..."* Or, *"I always wanted to..."*

Charity or Not?

A million pounds of bananas were purchased. They were shipped to the U.S. and given to a charitable organization. They were then shipped to Africa to feed the starving masses. By they time they got there they were rotten.

Million of dollars were donated to help people who were impacted by Hurricane Katrina. The main charitable organization that the money was given to did not use virtually any of the donate funds to help the victims of *Hurricane Katrina*. Instead, they kept it in the coffers, claiming they were waiting until it was needed.

On T.V. and radio commercials or when you are out and about, everyone seems to be asking you for a donation for a specific charity. They each claim that they are doing some good for the everyone and the everything. But, stations like CNN have done great documentaries about where the money you give these people actually ends up. And, in many, if not most cases, it never goes to the people, to the animals, or to the causes that the operators of the charitable organization claim that it is providing for. Instead, it ends up in their pockets.

That is a very sad state of affairs I think. But, I guess this type of con has been going on for time immemorial.

That fact is, within charities, people get paid to work there. There is a cap, at least here in the U.S., that the top dollar a person working at a charitable organization can make is two hundred and fifty thousand dollars a year. But, that's a lot of money. I would imagine that most of the people who donate to the organization do not make that kind of money per year. Yet, the people at the top pull in that kind of income – all from the donations of other people.

My question always has been, *"If they are taking money from other people to run their organization, why don't they do what they do there for free? If what their organization does is so good, that could be their contribution to the charity – free labor."*

Recently there had been a rash of the establishment of Non-Profit Organizations. Everybody seems to be setting one up. Once established the operators try to get investors to finances whatever cause their NPO is created around. But, similar to charities, most NPOs are set up simply as a means for the operator not to have to work, dodge taxes, and get money for free.

In both of these cases, people give. They give because they believe what they are giving to is a, *"Good Cause."* But, is it? No matter what you are told about a charity or a Not For Profit Organization, you need to factually find out where your hard-earned money is going and who is getting paid by you when you donate that money?

Yes Madam. Yes Sir.

There is a very simple fact in life, if you want to set your path for quick and unencumbered success you must play by the rules. You must dress conservatively, have a conservative hairstyle, act respectively and appropriately, say, *"Yes ma'am and yes sir,"* and never question authority.

Some people find this lifestyle very easy to live. They are taught from a young age to, *"Speak only when you are spoken to,"* and *"Respect your elders."* And, they do. They go to school, they get a job, and they do all the things that they are expected to do in the way they are expected to be done. They climb through the ranks as far as their background, education, determination, and circumstances will allow and that is their life. They have not rocked the boat and they have not caused controversy.

Is the life of a person who follows this path fulfilled; probably. They find their joy in the simple and the mundane. They are happy to provide for their family and they find happiness in the everyday aspects of life. They live a quiet, good life.

Some, particularly the young, when they look to the life of normality claim, *"I will never do that! I will never live my life in that manner!"* But, through circumstances and necessity most people end up following this path. Those who desired to pass through life differently are the ones who are unhappy with the cards life has dealt them. But, non-the-less, they fall into line and do what they must do.

The other path of life is much more complex. It is made up of those who question authority, create art, and even follow the path of criminality. For each of the people who choose these life paths, the one thing that they can be sure of is, their life will be much more complex, complicated, and insecure.

People hold onto the ideology that the life of an artist is somehow better. They believe this because they hear only about the few who have become very successful or those who have become well known after their death. Most artists fight through their entire life simply to survive and many spend their years living in depravation, starvation, and chaos. Though they are the ones who push the boundaries of society, they too are the one who pay the price for doing so. And, this does not just go for the painters; it goes to all levels of art: be it painting, writing, music, filmmaking, and everything else.

There is this illusion in the world that life is somehow better being on the outside of society. Certainly, when the artistic lifestyle if portrayed in films and in novels, it makes it look like even the struggle is fun and awe-inspiring. Though this is the portrayed image, most people who step onto the path can only handled it, even for a moment, if they are receiving money from their family or some other benefactor or they quickly leave behind the artistic lifestyle because poverty and starvation is never a fun place to dwell no matter how romantic the novels make it out to be.

The ways of the world are forever the winner. The fact is, the artists that actually make a good living at what they do are the ones who propagate the lie. They teach the wrong message, *"That everyone can be like me."* You can't. It just doesn't work that way. If you want to live a life of minimal struggle don't fight the world, give into it.

The Earth Still Spins

Whenever something traumatic or all-encompassing happens to you or something you care about, all of your attention is focused upon THAT. You are sad, you are upset, you are angry; you may even want to get revenge. What has happened has caused you to become very One-Pointed. But, no matter how much something that has happened to you or someone or something you care about may emotionally affect and control you, the earth still spins – the rest of the world goes on and no one else knows or even cares about how you feel.

This is one of the main things that you have to realize in life if you hope to pass through it with any level of refined consciousness. You have to understand that no matter how big the tragedy; other things are happening all across the globe that probably dwarf whatever happened to you.

Even in the case when some large catastrophe has occurred, most of the world still does not have a T.V or the Internet so even if they do hear about it, they cannot take the time to care, because they are surround by famine, by poverty, by violence, by war, or simply they need to go to work everyday to make ends meet. Thus, they cannot take the time to care.

People really get locked into their own head when they do not like what has happened to them or to someone whom they may care about. But, people can only behave in that manner, when they have the time, the money, and the emotional support to do so. They can only care when they do not have to worry about their own survival. They can only care when they have nothing better to do.

Think about this, if you have to focus on your own everyday survival would you care about the small things that you care about? Could you care about those things if you have no place to live, no food to eat, and no one to care that you care?

It really is a simply equation. And, you need to think about this before you spend the time and the emotional energy to be dominated by anything that is not Life-Essential.

Life is life. We pass though it. Things happen that we do not like to all of us.

Are you and your actions defined by those things? Or, are you more than that? Do they control you or do you control them?

Life and consciously living life on this planet is more than simply defined by how you feel about some event in the life of one person.

Seek something bigger than being focused upon you. That is *The Greater Pathway.*

Don't Do Things That Hurt People

Recently, I've been writing a lot about human interaction and how it affects humanity. In that vein, I was thinking back to a lecture I was asked to give on the subjecting of helping verses hurting a few years ago. After the lecture a number of people came up to me and said, *"Thank you. What you talked about really made me realize how the way I was behaving was not a good thing and I am going to change."* Though this was all well and good, I wondered if what I said was actually going to make people change, because people usually do not change their patterns unless something really big happens in their life that's makes them rethink their path. But then, as now, I always hope for the best.

We all know when what we are doing, or the way we are behaving, is bad. We all know when what we are doing is going to injure another person's life. Yet, there is this inner demon in many people that they cannot control. This may come from insecurity, childhood psychological trauma, desire, lust for power, unfulfilled dreams, or whatever... But, when these people get an idea in their head, they get adrenalized and they find a way to mess with someone or something. When this occurs, there is nothing that they can or will do to stop themselves. They have seen and they have conquered. They have made their point. They have gotten over on someone or something. They have won the battle. The problems is, when this style of confrontational mentality is embraced it makes the entire world a mess.

As most people who embrace this mindset are so engulfed in their own negative doing, they do not even think or care about how what they are doing is hurting the lives of others and, thus, damaging the overall energy of life. They do not think about it until the energy they have created comes back to haunt them. Then, generally, they still no longer think about how they have hurt others or this life-place because there are so wrapped up in what they are personally going though. There is no other word for this style of behavior but, *"Selfish."*

I have known people who have done a lot of negative things with their life and have hurt a lot of people along the way. Many of these people would justify their actions by stating that what they were doing was okay as it served them personally; made them feel the way they wanted to feel and caused them to live their life the way they wanted it to be lived. But, these people each eventually fell prey to their own negative karma.

I have also known a lot of people who lived in a space of self-sacrifice and giving. These people were able to live a life fairly free of confrontation and could be seen as having actually helped the world – even if they only did this in a very small way.

I cannot say this enough, *"Do good things. Don't do things that hurt people. Stop thinking only about yourself and try to understand how what you are doing is affecting others."*

It can be really invigorating to go after someone. Your thinking mind may even interpret it as fun. But, turn it around, understand the effect – how would it feel if what you are doing was happening to you?

Care! Care about people. Care about the earth. Care about life. You really need to care. That should be your first thought before you do anything else. And, don't do things that hurt people.

Everything Has Already Been Done

Whenever you throw your work or your ideas out there in the public, people are going to have thoughts about what you say or what you do. That's just life... For me, it forever amuses me when people take the time to watch one of my films, grab screen pulls from it, and then write a review totally bagging it due to Zen Filmmaking, lack of storyline, bad acting, crazy edits, weird credits, and all the etcetera...

Since I began making films over twenty years ago, my work has been reviewed a lot. It used to be predominately done in magazines and books, now it is on the Internet. All good... Kind of like what P.T. Barnum expressed, and Andy Warhol embraced, *"Any publicity is good publicity."* Well, maybe...

Anyway, what I have found is that the seasoned journalists and film reviewers get what I am doing. Many of the other people do not. Yet, they still take all the time to grab frames and write their thoughts.

Here's the thing... I'm an abstract artist. With that as a basis, it must also be understood that, everything has already been done. What I am attempting to do is something different. Defined by budgetary constraints, of course, do you not think that every element of all of my films are created with intent and focused consciousness? They didn't just happen. It was meant to be that way.

That being said, it actually amuses me to read the reviews that rip my films, because most of these reviewers do not take the time to understand what I am doing. If I may borrow a few words penned by the great Robert Allen Zimmerman, (Bob

Dylan), *"Don't criticize what you can't understand."*

The fact of the matter is, you can't come at something without understanding its basis or it just makes you look cretinous. If you want to go see a normal film then go to the movie theater and see whatever is on the big screen at the time. My films are intentionally not normal. Why even bother viewing them if you expect them to be like everything that has been done before? They are not. Creating seen-it-all-before visual arts was never my intention.

What I am saying is that... And, this goes to everything in life, not just films; before you draw a conclusion, you need to understand the basis, the focal point, and the reasoning behind a creation; once you know that, you can leave behind your personal ideologies and judgments and perhaps enter a new space of abstract understanding.

This is life; don't always base your opinions upon what you already know. Instead, take the time to turn off your mind and see things for what they are, not what you expect them to be.

And, like I have said forever, if you can make a better movie than me or anybody else why don't you quit wasting your time piggybacking on the creativity of other and writing reviews and instead get out there and do it, and let's see it.

Walk Around the Block

We all need to take a moment and walk around our block. We need to take a long hard look at where we area living and why. We need to see who we are.

Most people spend their entire life hiding. They hide from what they want from life, why they are doing what they are doing, and why they have given in to the ways of the world.

In Hinduism this is call, *Maya* – illusion.

But, with all the spiritual mumbo-jumbo aside, what is it that you want from life? Who is it that you want to be?

People forever make excuse for why they are not living the life that they desire. People forever blame all of the external circumstance for what has driven them to being who they are.

Who are you? Are you emulating all the good, all the understanding, all the knowledge that is within you? Or, are you just trying to play catch-up to the world that is spinning around you – telling you who and what you should be?

Take a moment right now. Take the time to take a walk around the block. Do this both physically and mentally – access who you are.

What is the result? The answer is yours.

What are you going to do about it?

Everything is Made in China

When I was a kid pretty much everything you purchased from cars to T.V.s, onto refrigerators, lamps, guitars, and everything else was, *"Made in the U.S.A."* There was the occasional radio or something that was, *"Made in Japan,"* but they were kind of thought to be somehow lacking, somewhat less.

The trend of items being creation in Japan continued and Japan became the place where pretty much all of the T.V.s and various other electronics were being produced. This process slipped by under the noses of the American populous, controlled by the corporations seeking to make bigger profits by producing their products in a less-expensive manner.

Then came the guitars... Japanese guitar makers began to be noticed in the 1970s when brands like *Ibanez* and *Takamine* began to make exact replicas of famous American guitars like the *Les Paul* and *Martin D40*. They were actually very well made guitars and sold for a fraction of the price of the U.S. editions. Me, I had an *Ibanez Double Neck,* serial number 13. Of course, the American companies owning the rights to these guitars sued these manufactures and the guitars created during this era ceased in creation and became known as, *"The Lawsuit Editions."* Now, they are very collectable.

The big blow, at least to U.S. made guitars, came when *Fender* and *Gibson* owned *Epiphone* began to make guitars in Japan in the 1980s. *"A Japanese Strat, can you believe it?"* Times and change continued and now these guitars are seen as very nice instruments.

The big shift came recently. I ordered a *Fender Strat* from *Musician's Friend*. I assumed it would be one of Fender, MIM, *"Made in Mexico,"* editions. But no, it was MIC, *"Made in China."* Fender has moved, at least some of their production, to China. Unbelievable... Using the *Fender* name, an icon of American craftsmanship, on a guitar created in the PRC.

For anyone who knows me, they know I have spent a lot of time in China. I have had quite a few experienced and adventures there – not all of them great... These exploits are spoken of in some of my novels and poetry. In any case, I have seen the PRC inside and out. I know its good points and I certainly understand its bad points. Long before China moved up to its forward position in world society, I predicated that they would someday rule the world. Why? Because they have a massive populous that is very afraid of the government – and from my experiences they should be. So, they have a cheap labor force, that is begging for work and, as such, producers from across the globe are drawn to them.

If you stay up on the news, even Apple has been accused of allowing the people who create their products in China to work and live under very exploitive conditions. And, that is just one of the large companies at the forefront of the news, there are many others.

Some people have gone on quests to only by, Made in U.S.A. products. I applaud them. But, that is not reality. Pretty much everything is made in China. And, it will continue to be so for the foreseeable future.

Good or bad is all a point of view. Better or worse, I don't know... But, we are only the people living in world controlled by whatever dominate influence holds the power. Today it is China, where everything is made. Just another phase of the Decline of Western Civilization. Welcome to the future where we will all be one race and there will be one controlling world power.

Art or Obsession?

Have you ever watched a person trim a bonsai tree? It is so precise that with every stroke you see perfection being etched. I have witness gardeners take this level of precise trimming technique to larger trees. It is pure beauty when they have finished. But, then what happens? The tree grows and all that they have done is lost. Is what they have done art or obsession?

Here in California there are some great artists who make beautiful sand sculptures on the shoreline. It takes them hour upon hour. Sometimes it is really amazing what they create. But then, the tide comes in and their art is washed away. Art or obsession?

In each of our lives I believe we have caught ourselves becoming obsessed with something that we are doing. For whatever reason we become so engulfed in what it is we are doing that even though we know what we do has little meaning to the overall expansion of human consciousness, we are fixated. I found myself doing just that this afternoon.

I have this rather large aquarium. I cleaned it yesterday and placed the rocks back in it – making tunnels for my fish to swim through and places for them to dwell. This afternoon I realized I didn't like the rock placement so I found myself spending quite a lot of time re-placing the rocks in just the right positioning.

My mind questioned, *"Is that right? No. Does this work? Maybe... No, I think this rock needs to be over there."* And, so on… I even found myself being a bit frustrated at times with the process. But then, it was done. It was right. Right, at least, to my mind's eye.

Now some may call this meditation. Some may call this perfectionism. Some may call this obsession. Some may even call this art. So, which is it?

…Because, at the end of the day, the rocks will again need to be moved when the aquarium is next cleaned. So, what I have done/what I have created is completely impermanent.

Art is the creation or the viewing of something that you personally find attractive and appealing. So, for me, in retrospect, what I was doing <u>was</u> creating art. Why? Because I liked the finished product. But, for others, they may think, *"That is terrible rock placement."* So, for them, it is not art.

Life, art, and even obsession is how you perceive it. To some, they may define meditation as an obsession. For others, they see it as their life's work. This is the same with art. People may not see the point or the purpose in the art created by others – whether it is designed to last for a moment or for an eternity. But, that does not make it any less of an artistic creation.

Obsession for art is the ultimate art. It is making the conscious decision to guide your life down the road to creation – no matter how temporary the art or your life may turn out to be.

Youth Is An Interesting Place

    Youth is an interesting place. But, you can never truly understand your youth until you look back upon it from the perspective of age.

    In youth, there is the belief that all of your dreams will come true. There is always the possibility of having it all. And, in youth, if it does not happen today, there is always tomorrow.

    In youth, love is everything. It will cure and heal all. You simply have to find it.

    All of these things and more define youth. But, what most young people do not yet comprehend is that the actions they take, the choices they make, define the rest of their life.

    I am often asked and I frequently discuss how essential it is to define the choices we each make in our lives. And, how the choices we make will define our future.

    In youth, *naiveté* generally defines all aspects of decision-making and personal choice. In youth, many young people have family support so they do not have to take a long hard look at their future and the true realities of living life until they are deep into what was once adulthood – their early twenties. From this, many choices and mistakes are made – choices and mistakes that can truly come to define a person's future.

    The fact of the matter is, not all of these choices are immediately life-altering. Often times, they are simple choices that set a course of events in motion that ultimately does not lead a person down the best path that their life could have followed.

    As I have long detailed, each of our lives are defined by available – by what is haveable and available to us. But, once the boundaries of these constraints are understood, we each move forward and form what is to become our future.

Most people would guide a young person to not do bad, evil, hurtful, and/or unlawful things. That's all pretty obvious. But, when one steps into the realms of subtleties like who to love, to advance one's education or not, where to work, what to wear, and how to behave; there it all get complicated for each of these elements will define one's future. And, there is no ultimate answer for how what you choose to do will affect what.

One thing I often suggest, as a means to view your possible future, is to investigate the road you are walking down by studying the lives of those who have walked it before you. And, not just those who were insanely successful at their endeavors while progressing down it; you also need to view what happened to the lives of the ones who failed at it, as well.

The one thing you have to contemplate when you are young (or old) is, *"How is what I am doing today going to affect my tomorrow?"* And, again, you may not know. You may be blind with love. You may believe you are walking on a path that will lead to a good livelihood. You may even think that by pursuing a career as an actor, artist, musician, you can contribute to society while living your artistic dreams. But, what you always have to question is what are the implications of your choices. What course of events will follow the choices you make today?

We all make mistakes. We all make choices and decision that, in retrospect, we should have gone a different direction – that's life. The main thing to keep in mind is to not let your youth fool you. Don't let your *naiveté* of today define your forever.

Think. Do not allow yourself to lie to yourself. Do not believe that simply because your currently have a supportive family that you will be allowed to live in the state of almost-adulthood forever. And, make good choices.

Be, as much as you can be in your moment. And, do not rush through or away from your youth.

Have You Hurt Somebody?

Have you hurt someone? Is what you are doing today going to hurt someone tomorrow? Did you hurt someone yesterday and is it still hurting them today?

Life begins with you. The world begins with you. Karma begins with you.

I forever find it very curious when somebody does something bad to another person and they don't care. They continue down their path without even thinking or caring about what they have done. Some never question, *"How did I damage that person's life by what I did?"* By not caring enough to ponder this, it illustrates that they do not possess the mindset to attempt to try fix what they have damaged. This is where all of the problems of the world begin.

Did hurting someone make you feel good? Did it make you feel powerful? Whatever your answer, think about this, *"How has it felt when someone hurt you?"*

My belief is that most people are good. They try to say and do good things and they try to help people when they see someone in need. There is another breed of person, however. They are the ones who do what they do and never even stop to think if they are hurting someone's life by what they have done. Then, if presented with the facts that they have hurt someone, they simply justify their actions.

This is the paradox of life. Most people who hurt people and then ignore or justify their actions are either too blank or too self-involved to even care what they have done. This is a very sad state of life.

You have to decide who you are in life because what you do today sets your next set of available circumstances in motion. If you hurt someone today and you do not care, what do you think your tomorrow will look like?

One of the most important things to realize in life is that the things you have broken can be fixed if you take the time to try. Repairing what you have broken makes everything better.

The beauty or the ugliness of the world begins with you. My belief is that you should make the world more beautiful.

Desire Verse Drive

There is a group of commercials currently in rotation where a kid of about ten is lecturing their younger siblings, *"Back in my day..."* Though this is an amusingly exaggerated example, as time passes on I believe we each have witness how things have become easier and more doable.

For example when I was a teenage musician, if I hoped to make an album I would have had to go into a recording studio, cut the record, and then have it pressed at a professional facility. All very-very expensive...

In recent years, there are a lot of people who have recorded an album on their computer in their apartment, put it on the Internet, and have become very successful. There are also some people who have simply made a video of themself singing a song, uploaded it to YouTube, and fame and success have happened.

In terms of filmmaking, when I began it was very-very expensive. The cost of the camera, the film, the sound equipment, the processing, and then the editing all were fairly astronomical. Now, you can buy a point and shoot camera go and film something, put it on the Internet, and there is a chance that your movie will open all kinds of doors for you.

There are a couple of people I have watched in recent years that have really taken this new level of relatively inexpensive technology and began to create their dreams. They have written and recorded music, gone out and made music videos to back up their songs. Some have gone out and made film shorts or even features. But, there is one element that is common among all of these people – they have done it.

All this being said, there is one very big reality about creativity. You have to do it. If you sit around and dream about something happening, it probably never will. You have to get out there and do it.

Does your Drive equal your Desire?

Chinatown Bong

I spent the past few days up in San Francisco. I was doing a commercial for a Japanese company. While I was there I also got to try out my new car camera mount as I filmed some footage for one of my upcoming films while driving around the city.

San Francisco is about five hundred miles north of L.A. I like the city and its surroundings. I spend a lot of time there. I've been going there ever since I was a little kid. I filmed movies there and I even wrote my undergraduate thesis on the history and urbanization of San Francisco's Chinatown. Which brings me to the point...

I was kicking around Chinatown the other evening after dinner with my lady. She makes jewelry and stuff and, as such, we occasionally hit a few of the shops in this tourist mecca due to the fact that have some interesting beads and the like.

The trends in Chinatown always change. They are a reflection of modern culture just like other places that sell vast amounts of junk to the public.

As I walked through the shops I began to notice that several of them had these really nice hand-blown glass bongs. It made me smile to think that the tourist from around the world would pick up their bongs in Chinatown.

Then I noticed something even more interesting. There were several shops that were selling these glass dope pipes, on a leather strand, to wear around your neck. Though they weren't all that big, they were pretty bulky and very obvious. It made me laughingly think, *"Who needs to get high so frequently that you need to wear a pipe around your neck?"* And, I think that kind or paraphernalia is even illegal in some places...

Anyway... These pipes also made me think back to the 70s when everybody was doing coke. Nobody thought it was addictive back then. It was just something that made you feel really-really good. Anyway, the Head Shops around Hollywood and other places all sold these nicely made coke spoons on chains so you could wear them around your neck – just in case you had the opportunity to grab a bump. But, they were pretty small and could be hidden inside your shirt. These pipes in Chinatown were big and obvious.

A funny side note here is, *McDonalds* used to create these coffee-stirring spoons back then. They were a long plastic white utensil with the *McDonald's* logo the top and a little spoon for mixing in the crème and sugar at the bottom. The spoon was the perfect size for grabbing a hit of coke and everybody had one lying around. *McDonalds* eventually figured out what was going on and changed them to simply having a larger flat edge where the spoon used to be. Just a piece of history for the cultural history books...

Though the pipes sold in Chinatown are fully functional, I realized that maybe they are more for the young adolescents who want to own and announce that they are Stoners then for the people who really need them to get high. Adolescences seems to be the time in life when you want to scream the loudest about who and what you are. The problem is, even though pot is all but legal in California and some other places, if you call attention to yourself, (for all the wrong reasons), it can set a course of events in motion in your life that can set the stage for ruination. I knew a lot of people who were young like I in the 70s, who loudly announced who and what they were and ended up in jail, simply because of loudly announcing who they were and what they were doing; which lead to more time in jail, which then lead to even more time in jail, which ultimately lead to a life with no way back.

    Play dress-up if you want. Own who are, that's all fine. But, if being who you are crosses the norms of society be ready to pay the price.

Martial Arts on the Spiritual Path

People on the spiritual path commonly ask me how could I be involved in something so seemingly violent as the martial arts. Martial artists continually ask me why do I place such an emphasis on spirituality. Though these two venues seem worlds apart, they are, in fact, closely inter-linked.

For those of us who are old enough to remember the 1970's television series, *"Kung Fu,"* where Kwai Chang Cane, a Shao Lin monk, was living in the Old West and continually flashing back to the lessons he learned while living at the Shao Lin Temple, we were presented with a standard whereby the average individual could sense a correlation and seeming necessity for even the most spiritual of persons using hand-to-hand combat. Though this television series was a theatrical presentation and historically inaccurate, it did define that there has long been martial artists in Asia who have been closely linked to their spirituality.

First of all, however, it must be defined that every individual or martial arts practitioner who lives or comes from Asia is not necessarily an enlightened being. This is one of the common pitfalls many westerners fall into believing when they go to train in the martial arts. They think simply because a person hails from Asia they somehow know more, are more, and should be universally revered as such.

Throughout Asia, just as in the West, there are those individuals who are drawn to the spiritual path and embrace it. And, just like in the West, there are far more people who only care about self, wealth, personal prestige, and couldn't care less about spirituality – though due to their geographical upbringing they oftentimes have picked up more facts about eastern religion than is commonly possessed by a Westerner.

This being stated, due to the fact that the origin of the martial arts was based in Asia, eastern religion came to be the philosophy adhered to by the spiritually inclined practitioner of these systems of self-defense. As such, it was eastern religion that came to be the defining factor of the spiritual basis for the martial arts.

An important factor to keep in mind when considering the link between martial arts and spirituality is that the two predominate religions which came to directly influence the martial arts are Taoism and Buddhism. Both of these philosophies are intrinsically defined with a deeply meditative and metaphysical process of thought. Religions of the West, such as Christianity and Islam, though no less viable conduits of faith, are not delineated by these characteristics. An example of this is that they do not commonly send the practitioner down the road of attempting to loose the Personal Self in order to gain a glimpse of the Cosmic Whole.

As the martial arts have continued to evolve throughout the centuries, so too have the various sects which make up Taoism and Buddhism. To this end, as time has progress some schools of the Chinese and Japanese martial arts have come to be keenly linked to their various philosophic traditions. Certainly, such arts as Tai Chi, through in actually a martial arts based on physical deflections, punching and kicking, is now seen as an essential form of movement meditation. This is no less the case with such Japanese systems of martial arts as Iaido, where a practitioner draws his sword in an exacting manner, delivers a precisely orchestrated technique, and then returns the sword to its sheath in a definitively meditative manner.

From these two illustrations we can see the martial arts do not have to solely be a method to kick butt. They can be a means for the body and mind to move into a state of exacting harmony, whereby the practitioner is removed from the constraints of physical existence and may gain a glimpse of meditative consciousness.

Though the martial arts are based in techniques of physical confrontation, that does not have to be their ending point. They can become something much-much more.

One of the key problems embraced by the modern martial artist is the fact that they are taught in their martial art schools to live their life from a very competitive perspective. They are taught to believe that their style, their instructor, and, in fact, they are the best at what they do. What this causes, as can be noted by anyone who has been involved in the martial arts for any length of time, is the fact that there is an enormous amount of back stabbing, criticizing, and a general sense of hypocrisy going on among practitioners from differing styles or schools. What this leads to is a life embraced by competition that is completely absent from peace.

If you live your life at the level of constantly seeking confrontation, attempting to find a reason to battle with the hopes of overpowering or defeating anyone or everyone, for whatever reason, you are forced to live your life from a very animalistic perspective. And, like I have long said, just like the gun fighters of the Old West, there will always be somebody faster. Eventually you will be defeated.

To the person who lives their life at this level, they are constantly being engaged in confrontations and battles that are finding them out of the blue. Why? Because they are projecting a sense of confrontation to the universe – what you sew is what you reap.

Though the modern martial arts commonly breeds this style of aggressive, competitive mindset, this does not have to be the case. Just as the practitioners of Tai Chi or Iaido have proven, the martial arts can be a great source of movement meditation – where there is no need for conflict.

The essential thing to remember is that the essence of movement meditation is not defined by what style of martial arts you practice – though, obviously, certain styles are more open to having a students become meditative in their movements than others. None-the-less, it is you who possess the ability to raise your martial arts to the level where something more than physical or mental conflict is embraced.

From the martial arts you learn to protect yourself if the need arises. But, fighting does not have to be the end point of your training.

If you are not seeking unnecessary conflict, you are not tracked down by it. If you are living your life embracing the glory of your existence, by whatever religious or philosophic criteria you choose, you will not be bound by the limitations of other martial artists you encounter that are hell bend on making themselves appear to be bigger, better, or more by whatever title, award, lie, or punch they possess. If you live your life from a focus of consciousness, you can transcend the limitations of any situation you encounter. This will naturally occur not by fighting your way out, but by experience all of life from a state of universal understanding.

Are the martial arts violent? Only if you let them be.

That's Life/That's Work

Starbucks is about to changes its whole food menu. In August they are going to introduce soups, all kinds of new fresh, warmed up, bakery items, and all kinds of other new stuff. I know this because I am an over-the-counter friend with the manager of my local *Starbucks.*

I have been a big fan of *Starbucks* ever since they hit L.A. in '91. The first one was located at the Beverly Connection – which is across the street from the Beverly Center in West Hollywood/Beverly Hills. A pretty young lady I was hanging with at the time introduced me to *Starbucks* when my friend Don Jackson and I had a editing suite in an industry office building connected to the Beverly Connection. We were housed there as we edited *The Roller Blade Seven.*

Awh, the parties that went on in that editing suite... One of our friends of a friend came in one evening and questioned, *"Does stuff like this really go on?"* My answer was, *"Yes it does..."*

Anyway, I got hooked on *Starbucks.*

... Have you ever visited the first *Starbucks* in Seattle? How this coffee megalopolis has grown from that small store is beyond me. Anyway, to the point...

Being friends with the manager of my local *Starbucks,* today he reminded me that he plays softball. His team made it to the World Series of softball to be held in Washington D.C. this year. The problem is... When is it? August, when *Starbucks* will be making their major shift. The powers that be told him he can't go. He has to be in his store.

Can you believe it? Making it to the World Series and you can't go. How messed up is that? I mean, most of us dream our whole life of being in just one World Series or something similar. This guy has the chance and his job won't let him go.

I told this story to a friend of mine. She said, *"That's life, that's work."*

Maybe… But, I think it is really sad that our jobs have to dominate so much of our lives. They have us trapped, for without them, how can we survive? But, with them, they have the potential to rob our dreams.

Is Painting an Accomplishment?

To the artists, there is little they would rather do than paint. But, as has long been discussed, art, like beauty, is in the eye of the beholder.

An artist paints and creates art, because that is what they do. To the non-artist they look at art and judge it as to whether or not they like it. *"This is good. That is bad..."*

But, art can only be judged and/or appreciated when it has been created. If no one created art, then there would be no discussion of art.

To many artists, they paint but they do not try to exhibit their work. They paint because they love to paint – they find it relaxing, creative, cathartic, and a million other things. But, artists also judge themselves. Many do not believe that what they are creating is GOOD enough for others to see their work.

When I have a moment, my distraction has long been to go to thrift stores, because you never know what kind of cool vintage items or cultural memorabilia you will find within their walls. One of things I have long noticed is that there is a lot of art that has been given away. Some of it is painted in fashion that I would consider not done by a developed artist. But, I have also found art pieces by very established and in some cases well-known artists. So, just because it is discarded does not mean that it is not created from a perspective of excellence.

Art is not limited to painting. Music is art. Yet, many people only play their music within the confines of their own home.

I think back to a realization I had in the 1980s. One of my longstanding friends owns a music shop. Back in the 1980s a lot of the L.A. based super groups frequented his shop. Everybody from *Ratt,* to *Dokken,* to *Great White,* onto *Guns and Roses* used to rehearse in the rear studio while he repaired and customized their guitars in the front. Aside from the rock stars there were also a lot of simple musicians that used to come through the doors. (The shop was a real hangout place back then). In any case, I realized that some of the best guitar players I ever met never made it to rock star level at all. They were simply super-masterful guitarists who played within much smaller confines, many never played in public at all.

Kind of like the old Zen proverb goes, *"If a tree falls down in the wood and there is no one to hear it, does it make a sound?"*

This questions goes to art and music. If someone creates art and does not get it out there to the public, is it art – is what they have done an accomplishment?

My belief is, yes it is. In fact, it may be more of an accomplishment because it is done from a much purer space than simply seeking the admiration and/or the financial rewards given by the masses.

If art is created simply as art, then it is pure. If a guitar is strummed in a bedroom, the beauty of it is allowed to exist in a space of solitude – meditatively focusing and soothing the mind of guitarist; pianist, flautist, whatever…

So, is painting an accomplishment if no one but the artist ever sees it? Yes it is.

You Weren't There So You Don't Know

I often become very amused, (and even occasionally annoyed), when I read stories that people have written about what took place during the creation of some of my films. These people have these whole elaborate dialogues taking place. The only problem is, they are universally wrong.

Those actions were never taken. Those words were not spoken. Those ideas were not discussed. And, those ideologies were never attempted to be actualized.

People have even gone as far as to write entire articles amount my films, my self, and my filmmaking partners – all in an attempt to totally berate and slam me. Dudes... If you are going to do that, at least get your facts straight!

You know, there has been something truly lost with the creation of the Internet. Sure, a lot has been gained. Everybody who wants to have one, can have a voice. And, that is great. But, what has been lost is the quest for TRUTH. People say anything, and they do not even care if they are right, wrong, lying, or simply presenting what they think and wish occurred. It all is sounded with the same voice and it is all consumed without the presence of mind to confirm whether or not what a person wrote possesses any validity.

People hide behind the mask of fan, film geek, reviewer, intellectual, whatever... But, by whatever name they assign themselves, what they propagate is falsehoods hidden behind the guise of someone who has actually taken the time to write something. And, once they write what they write, someone else reads it and believes it, thus the lie is perpetuated.

The number one thing I have to say in response is, I spend my time creating self-developed art. What do you spend your time doing?

People… You weren't there, so you don't know. Stop writing about a subject where you have no factual basis for your conclusions.

Tell Them Willy Boy Is Here

I was kicking back at home tonight, Saturday late-night, flipping through the channels and I found the movie, *"Tell Them Willy Boy Is Here."* I had to watch it.

It is a great movie starring: Robert Blake, Robert Redford, Katherine Ross, and Susan Clark. It came out the same year as, *"Butch Cassidy and the Sundance Kid,"* which also starred, Robert Redford and Katherine Ross.

Which one came first, I do not remember. I will leave that to the film historians... But, both are essential films.

I remember seeing, *"Tell Them Willy Boy Is Here,"* (and *Butch Cassidy*), at the Wiltern Theater here in L.A. back in '69. I was just a kid but already deeply involved in film.

At the time of this film's release, there was a lot of attention being brought to the plight of the Native Americans and the trails and tribulation they had been put through via the invasion of their lands. I remember very clearly feeling for the plight of Willy Boy and his love Lola, played by Katherine Ross, when originally watching the film.

Many years later, Robert Blake went thought his own societal domination brought about by who he was, what he was, and his quest for love and/or whatever else you may define the relationship that lead to his demise...

Back in the day, as a young teenager, I remember watching him on *The Johnny Carson Show*, rambling about his career, his mental illness, and whatever else crossed his mind. He was very entertaining. A true artist disturbed by all that life had feed him from his emersion as a child actor on the, *"Our Gang,"* series, forward through his stunning cinema work, onto the television series, *"Baretta,"* that my bud Saturday Jim and I used to have to cut our evenings short on Friday night to get home to watch.

Shortly after the release of the film, *"Tell Them Willy Boy Is Here,"* I moved from my first instructor and began working out at this new martial arts studio in the Koreatown section of L.A. For whatever reason, there were a lot of Native American students frequenting that studio. From them, I began to experience true exposure to the life, life styles, and the experiences of the American Indians in the United States. I even became close friends with a few of them.

Many years later, during the days of filming, *"The Roller Blade Seven,"* I met a very nice person, who also was Native American. She played the Spirit Guide in the film. We became very close, at least for a moment... Great lady!

From all of these relationships, I gained a deeper understanding of what the Native Americans have been forced to experience in order to make their way through this modern world. In many cases, these experiences have been anything but ideal.

By the 1980s, concern about the conditions that many Native Americans still face on a daily basis had faded from the forefront of modern consciousness. In this modern era, I think that most Americans do not even ponder the current plight of the Native Americans. I believe this is very sad.

If you take the time to view a very good movie like, *"Tell Them Willy Boy Is Here,"* and if you look beyond the obvious of the film, you are really allowed to see how the Native Americans were cast to a world where they could not win and could not even truly survive and thrive by what WE, the American people's, have done to them.

Hell, the primary characters of the film were not even played by Native Americans…

Perhaps as an interesting change of fate, over the past decade or so, many tribes across the United States have began to open casinos on their land as they are Federal and can sidestep local laws about gambling. The character Willy Boy in the film was from the Morongo tribe. In recent years this tribe has opened one of the most successful casinos in Southern California near Palm Springs. I don't know how much of the money made by this casino is used to aid the lives and the livelihood of the members of this tribe but I am sure it has helped.

Though gambling is never good due to the fact that people have the potential to lose everything. It does seem somewhat karmicly interestingly that the Native Americans have finally found a way to reestablish themselves, beating their invaders at their own game.

Thank You For Your Kindness

How does it feel when someone goes out of his or her way to help you? It feels pretty good, doesn't it?

Maybe they go out of their way to help you for no good reason. They just do it. With this, it let's you know that there is still hope for humanity.

Most of us understand how it feels when we get the help we need, when we need it. Yet, this does not motivate many of us to go out into life doing good things and actually thinking about helping others.

Most people are stunk in themselves. If they get help when they need it, great! But, they never try to return the favor.

I believe people should start rethinking their lives. Get out there and do good things. They don't have to be big. Just help people when they need it and this whole Life-Place will become better.

Yesterday I went to the PCC (Pasadena City College) Flea Market. I parked a couple of blocks away. When I returned to my car there were literally hundreds of motorcycles gathered around it – both on the street and on the sidewalk. They were all old Nortons, BSAs, and Triumphs. It must have been some sort of British motorcycle club. I get to my car and there was only a few inches to the front and to the back of it. My first thought was, *"Fuck me, how am I going to get out of here."* I let my lady in the car and just as I was walking to the driver side a guy runs up, *"Let me help you get out of here, man." "Thanks!"* He was my outside eyes and guided my car back and forth, to be ready to pull out. What he did totally turned what could have been a bad experience into a very nice one. All he did was step up and help.

A funny side note was, just as I was making my final pull out to the street, a cop pulls up right next to me with his lights flashing. I look at him with a small smile and point to indicate that I was about to pull out. The cop in the passenger seat, in all the bravado that some cops possess, exclaims, *"I'm not going anywhere. I here for this!"* It reminded me of why so many people dislike cops, the rude, all-empowered, arrogance, that some of them posses.

Back when I used to operate a martial art studio I taught a lot of law enforcement professionals self-defense. Most of them were really nice guys who did their job with passion. A few were like this cop, however, rude and arrogant.

You know, being a cop is the most empowering blue-collar job a person can get.

After speaking to me, he continues forward yelling from the car at the motorcycle riders about being parked on the sidewalk and so on. The cop in the driver seat must have been one of the better breed. He pulled up a little bit to let me pull out. I was on my way.

This is an ideal example of life. There are those who go out of their way, even just a little bit, and they truly help the on-goings of life. Others want to power-trip and block the flow. We each know which one is better. Get out there, do small things, (or big things), stop only thinking about yourself, and help people!

Everybody Wants a Better Life

When people view the lives of other people, universally it is believed that some other person has a better life. Maybe that is true. There are some people with more money, more success, they drive a better car, they have a better job, they live in a better house in a better location, they are happier, they are more enlightened, and all of that kind of stuff. But, this is not the end-all...

Everybody, no matter how rich, how successful, how whatever, wants a better life.

Like I forever have detailed, *"There is always a price to pay..."* In everybody's life, for every choice and decision you make, for every step you take, for everything you do, <u>there is a price to pay</u>.

Some of the choices you make lead to a better life. Maybe you were simply born into a very wealthy family and, as such, many doors were opened for you. But, whatever the case, everybody is stuck in this Life-Place and no one is fully universally content with their life. We all want more. We all want better. We all want to be free of the pains that haunt us. We all want to be free of the people that do bad things around us.

You can run but you can't hide. We are stuck. This is life.

This is why renunciation has called out to so many people over the centuries. They have left the ways of the world for the spiritual path because they simply no longer wanted to deal with all the common Life-Stuff anymore. In many traditions, this is the idealized place to be and the best way to live your years – leave it all behind...

I have long discussed some of the perils of the spiritual path and how, even while walking upon it, you still encounter people and are forced to deal with their personalities and their individual idiosyncrasies. So, I am not going to discuss that here. But, I will say, just as urbanization has continued to shrink our world's natural environment, so too has it closed in on the realms of spirituality. There's no place left to run... So, getting away and leaving it all behind is just not really doable anymore. Yeah, you can find somewhat of a shelter but it is not absent from the constraints of the modern world as it once may have been.

So, what to do? You simply must accept that you are not going to have it all. No matter how far up the financial ladder you may climb, and no matter how much of your precious Life-Time you take pursuing your wants, your life is never going to be perfect as long as you hold onto the desire of, *"Better."* So, stop giving into the belief, *"If only I had that..."* Or, *"If I could live like that person then I would be happy."* Because everybody, no matter how successful, wants more. Everybody wants better. Everybody wants something different. Everybody wants the bad that occurs in all of our lives to go away.

Ultimately, if you want your life to be better, stop thinking only about yourself and stop doing things that hurt other people and negatively affect this world we live in. Instead, start doing things that help. Then, even if only for a moment, you will stop being self-involved and you may actually make this Life-Place a little bit happier – a little bit, *"Better."* From this, in that moment you and the people you have helped will not desire to be living a better life.

Better is already in you.

Friend or Foe

I forever find it interesting in life how people perceive themselves as friends with another person only to find out that their friend backstabbed them without a second thought. Certainly, this has happened to me more times than I would choose to remember as I am sure it has happened to most of us. But, there is one commonality involved in this process and that is the primary reason for why this style of behavior takes place; most people are very self-involved, very self-serving, and only think about how they are feeling in their own moment. They never take the time to consider how their actions affect the life of the person they are deceiving and how that action will affect their own Life-Unfoldment.

By my nature, I see everyone as a friend. I always have. That is simply who I am. I continue to hold that assessment about a person until I am shown that I was wrong.

Stepping back from myself, I do not believe that is a bad trait. Perhaps if more people were like that, the world would be a better and friendlier place. But, that is not how it is. People are our forever out for themselves. They are most commonly your friend because you have something that they want.

I have witnessed this so many times in my life. People stalk me, pretending to randomly bump into me, or call me time-after-time, and all kinds of stuff like that... They do this not to be a true friend but because they want to be involved in one of my films or one of my other projects. The thing is, all they would have had to do is ask, I would have been happy to bring them on board. But, they go about it in a totally different way, appearing to be friends but basing their actions upon ulterior motives.

I believe this example is a very common pattern in most people's lives. People reach out to them because they want something – whatever that something may be.

I have also witnessed people fiercely turn on me for no reason. They have done this when I was the only one to ever go out of my way and actually try to help them achieve their dreams and desires. Why they behave like this is anybody's guess. It is just an aspect of their personality, I suppose. And, I am sure that they would each have a reason. But, by approaching life and the helping-hand of another in this manner, what they did was to destroy the future they could have had. They end up back where they were instead of on a path of self-fulfilling creativity. As the years have gone on, several people have contacted me, expressing that they wish they had handled themselves differently as they have seen the results of where their life-path has lead.

From my own perspective of friendship, I forever try to bring something to the table to offer. And, if someone is ushering me down a road to betterment via our friendship, which has happened a number of times, I am forever thankful.

I think the main thing about friendship that you must keep in mind is that, simply because you like a person and/or are friends, that does not mean that they are the same as you. Though you may meet and interact in a particular space, they may very-well may be living their life from a completely different perspective than you – based upon a completely different set of desires and life experiences.

You are you. They are who they are. You need to be able to meet in the middle and not attempt to force that person to be anything other than what they are.

If you choose to associate with a person, and that is a choice only you can make, that does not mean that you control them. By letting a person be who they are, that is the basis of true friendship. If they do something you don't like – that's life! That is just the way it is. The fact of the matter is, everybody, sooner or later, is going to do something you don't like. Friendship means you accept that.

But, there is also a *code of honor* attached to friendship. If a so-called friend lies to you, consciously deceives you, or is guiding your life in a bad direction, it is time to end that association and move away. Friendship is a two-sided experience.

Too Famous.
...For All the Wrong Reasons.

I had an audition early this week for a Midwestern commercial. They had only called in a few people for the audition. I believe there were four others and myself. So, this was a tight call. A lot of times production companies will see hundreds of actors for a role. For this one, that was not the case – they were seeking someone with a very specific look.

A kind of interesting thing happened to me at that audition. I went in and they slated me. That is where they take a digital photo of you, they do an upward pan of your body, you show your profiles, and you tell them your name. All common stuff...

In the room of this casting session was the cameraman, (doing the filming), and over on the couch were the director and a couple of other people. They were probably representatives from the company that this commercial was being created for.

In any case, as always occurs, the cameraman asked for my name. *"Scott Shaw,"* I reply. I noticed when I said my name a guy on the couch nudged the director and gave a little point. He whispered, *"That's Scott Shaw..."* They looked at each other and then at me. Once the cameraman was done with his duties I receive a question from the director,

"You're Scott Shaw?"
"Yes."

A strange look comes over his face, and a moment or two passes.

"I really liked your book, "Zen O'clock."
"Thanks."

At that moment, I knew I was not going to get the gig. I knew this even though I still went through the motions and read for the role...

Obviously what had happened is that my agent had submitted me and the casting director had brought me in due to my appearance. But, the casting director probably didn't read my name.

Here's the thing... Everybody who is not a part of Hollywood believes that fame and accomplishment is the end-all. Let me tell you, it is not. In fact, many times it works against you.

For example, this role called for a New Age Guru type. All good, I look the part. But, the problem is, they could never cast me because then it would look like the company was endorsing my books and me. Thus, I lost the role.

This is the same thing for the type of films that an actor does. For example, when I first stared out in the industry, (at the ripe old age of thirty-two), I initially worked in A-market roles or on indie films that were geared towards the mainstream. When Don Jackson decided he wanted me to star in *Roller Blade Seven*, I knew my career would be changed forever. Though that style of film was and is much more in-tune with how I see the cinematic arts, it is the kind of film that sets a precedent for your career. In fact, my friend Joe Estevez once said to me about *Roller Blade Seven*, "I'm surprised either of our careers survived after doing that film."

That is true. That film and that style of filmmaking has defined me, in the film industry, since the day it was released. Though I have occasionally been brought in to do roles in mainstream films, T.V., and commercials here in the States since RB7, those castings were more based upon the way I looked rather than the anti-fame I gained from that film and the other Zen Films I have created.

This is an important thing to understand about Hollywood. The casting directors are not seeking talent. They are either going to cast people that are sent to them by powerful agents, who set the standards and pretty much define the film game, or people who have a very specific look needed for a specific role.

Though this is the case with Hollywood, Asia is a bit of a different story. For the most part, the powers-that-be there do not view the kind of films I make as a detriment. They simply see them as Comic Book Action Adventures. A style of film that is very common throughout Asia. And, my films have done very well there.

This being stated, the other side of the coin is that due to the type of films I make, I continually receive offers to be in obscure indie films made by other filmmakers. I always turn those offers down, however. As I forever jokingly state, *"The only bad films I'm in are my own."*

Plus, I believe Joe Estevez is the king of that genre. I certainly do not want to infringe upon his territory.

Ultimately, fame and notoriety is an evil master. I remember back when Dennis Rodman was just veering off from the top of his game. He had done a film with Mickey Rourke and Jean-Claude Van Damme. Though around this time he had been released from the Lakers, he was still everywhere – all over the media. Some reported asked him, *"Why don't you get more film and television work?"* He replied, *"Because I'm too famous."* He would later use this same statement to define why the courts severally punished him for his illegal deeds. Maybe that is true. I don't know. But, it is true that fame, no matter from which area it comes, defines your life and it keeps you from moving forward because you will forever be defined by that definition.

In terms of Rodman, I'm glad he has found success in Reality T.V. And hey, he's now a friend with the leader of North Korea. :-)

Anyway, it is important to think about what you are doing. Many people come to Hollywood and only focus upon the A-Industry. I wish them all the best, but that is a near impossible nut to crack. As for the world of indie, the opportunities are greater if you have a look or a skill or if you are a woman willing to take off her clothing. But, whatever you decided to do, remember; once it is out there in the public eye; it is out there forever. Any noteworthiness or fame you obtain will define you. And, that will dictate your next set of available opportunities.

Seeing Who You Don't Want To See

Don't you hate it when you bump into someone you don't want to see? Maybe you are walking down the street, in a restaurant, having a latte' at a café, whatever... Then, out of nowhere, they appear.

There are all kinds of reasons why you may not want to see a person. Maybe you don't like them. Maybe they are weird. Maybe they bother you. Maybe there has been some weirdness that went on between the two of you. But, then you see them and the intimal thought is to try to avoid eye contact. Maybe they won't notice me... And, all that. But, no matter how it plays out, the situation is always going to be strange.

There is the other side of this situation, however. When someone, out of nowhere, comes up to you, from somewhere deep in your past, and it is good to see them.

This happened to me a couple of years back. An old friend I had met in San Francisco back in '76 had contacted me. She hit me up via email and I made the drive up there. It was great to see her again. We eventually lived out a bit of unfinished karma and it was all-good...

The weirdest thing happened on our first re-meet, however. She set up our rendezvous at this weird, what I felt was dirty, hippie restaurant. Hate hippies! Take a bath and move into the twenty-first century... Anyway, I couldn't eat there. Too dirty... But I had a coffee. Post that session we were standing outside conversing a little bit further and I notice a big burly guy standing behind me. I mean this guy was build like a brick shit-house. I turned around and looked at him. *"Scott... Scott Shaw?"* I didn't answer but continued to look.

Living in the world I live in, I have to be a bit paranoid. I was thinking, re: being asked to meet the girl at that restaurant and everything, *"Who is this. And, just what is going on?"*

In any case the guys says, *"It's me..."* I'm going to omit his name. But, he was and is a great guy. He had helped my out all kinds of ways back in the early 90s with taking photographs for my martial art articles and helping me film some of my early movies. I hadn't seen him in years. Had no idea he moved from L.A. to S.F.

It was just that weird style of karmic reality. The guy had an office right next to the restaurant this girl had asked me to meet at.

We spoke for a few minutes, I told him about the fact that this actress I had introduced him to many years the previous had recently contacted me via MySpace.

Again, this was strange... Of all the people that had come and gone via my involvement in the film industry, this blonde bombshell, (and I use this as a very exact description of her), she was the only person I ever wondered what had happened to. One day she was just gone. This guy, like I, assumed she might have passed on to the next world. But no, she was living in the South.

Anyway, it was great to see the guy. Out of nowhere... It was great to re-meet my friend from the past. It was great to hear from the actress – a compatriot from so long ago. This was all kind of like the opposite of the blog I wrote a few weeks ago titled, *"People Fall Away."*

Bumping into someone. I don't know... Maybe it is a chance, maybe a last chance, to change the dynamic, reform the karma? Or, maybe it is just a jab from the cruel hands of fate?

Whatever it is, bumping into someone from the past, whether you want to see them or not, is what you make of it.

Something is Lost in the Recording

Back in about '78 I had the chance to see *The Ramones* open a concert for *Black Sabbath* at the Long Beach Arena. Today, that paring seems pretty bizarre. And, I guess it was. For me, it was the perfect combination as it was a depiction of how my musical tastes had shifted from one genre to another.

I was part of the first wave of the new wave – punk rock. Back when bands like *Patti Smith* and *The Ramones* were changing the way music was interpreted and bands like *The Weirdo's, The Germs, The Slits, Black Flag,* and *The Dickies* were reshaping music altogether. All this after groups like *Iggy and the Stooges, MC5,* and before them, *The Sonics,* had laid the foundation for this style of music to happen.

Anyway, there was one thing that occurred during the *Black Sabbath* segment of that show that blew me away. The band left the stage leaving Tony Iommi playing his guitar. He stood there alone for ten, fifteen minutes; whatever... Just tearing it up. As a guitar player I was simply blown away by his chops. Whenever I have relayed this story to my guitar player aficionado friends, they always state, *"That never came across on the albums."* And, that's true.

Recently, I picked up a rather obscure *Black Sabbath* live CD, Past Lives. I was hoping it would capture some of that guitar magic I remember. To a degree it does, but there is unfortunately none of that ongoing, nonstop, several minutes of guitar mastery presented on it. But, it does let the listener hear the *Black Sabbath* that was – back then...

I feel like Tony Iommi is similar to Frank Zappa, another masterful guitarist, whose albums never captured that mastery. You really had to see him live to witness it. But, he was great!

From a personal perspective I can kind of understand the process and the result. Whenever I have recorded, I too have found it difficult to capture those perfect moments of guitar playing that occur when the tape is not rolling. Even when I have been playing something, thought is was great, and immediately went and recorded it – the moment the mic was in-place or the guitar plugged in, and the tape or the digital recorder was rolling – the music that came out, just was not the same.

I guess somehow there is a Zen perfection in all of that/this. Those perfect moments when you are simply playing and IT happens. And then IT is lost to the realms of the Akashic Record forever.

Perfect moments can rarely be recorded...

Claiming Spirituality

Some people are drawn to the Spiritual Path. Some are not. Some people are herded onto the spiritual path by family members or friends, but if it is not who they truly are, they leave as soon as they find an exit.

Being on the spiritual path is like anything else in life, if it is who you are then you wish to tell others about it. You wish to inform others about your involvement on it, your understandings gained from embracing it, and what it has to offer the all and the everybody.

There is a very big problem once you claim spirituality, however. You are then judged as either behaving spiritually or the opposite.

If you claim spirituality you are expected to behave in a certain manner. And, though each religion and spiritual group will each embrace their own unique understanding about what is or is not spiritual – if you claim it, you will be judged as to whether or not you are actually living and embracing it.

If you claim spirituality you are essentially stating that you do not possess any of the common traits expressed by the masses: no anger, no frustration, no desire, no lust, no ego, and all of that kind of stuff. The problem is, most people who claim spirituality are not spiritual. They are simply using whatever knowledge they may have gained from learning something about the metaphysical aspects of life and using it to make themselves seem like, *"Something."* But, if you are, *"Something,"* you never have to tell anyone that is who or what you are. It will simply be obvious

It's pretty cool to be spiritual, isn't it? It's pretty cool to be able to tell people what they should do and how they should live, isn't it? These and more are all motiving factors for claiming spirituality.

To be truly spiritual, however, you never claim spirituality. You simply live. You try to do good things. You try to say good things. You try not to behave inappropriately. And, if you do, you apologize to anyone you may have offended. If someone asks you for guidance, you silence your opinions and tell them to look inside themselves for the answer.

Being spiritual is not claiming to be spiritual. It is accepting this Life-Condition and living just like everyone else. You simply try to do it with a refined sense of consciousness that can only be had when you claim nothing.

Monkey Wrench in the Gears

Life goes along for most of us quite expectedly. We do what we do. And, though we may not always be *Thriving,* we are *Surviving.* Most of life is Okay.

Then, out of the blue we are hit with an unexpected sucker punch to the back of the head. Something goes really wrong. This may occur on all kinds of levels: interpersonal, mechanical, or a natural disaster. From this, a monkey wretch really gets thrown into the gears of our life and everything becomes a mess.

First of all, this is JUST life. Like the only saying goes, *"Shit happens."* No one is immune. The more involved and complicated your life, however, the more chance you have of having a monkey wrench thrown into your gears. On the other hand, the less you do, the less chance you have of unexpected occurrences.

This is why the *Tao Te Ching* states, *"To the man of the world, everyday something is acquired. To the man of Tao, everyday something is lost."*

By consciously stepping away from the world and the ways of the world, not only does your life become more passive and clear, it also becomes less prone to obstacles. But, the reality is; life is life. We all seek our own form of involvement. We all need human interaction. And, we all need to do THINGS. From these things is where chaos is born.

So, what is the answer? Many on the spiritual path continually attempt to step farther and farther away from the world. But, as a living being, we are all going to die. This too is a monkey wrench in the gears. Because, we each have things we would like to accomplish, complete, actualize, or witness at the time of our death. This is one of the primary curses of life. If we continually step away, attempting to refine ourselves to the degree that we believe we are free from consequences; all that will be had is life left unlived and a death full of regrets.

The trick, the key if you will is to be able to step back from any crisis that befalls you. Don't attribute it to god testing you or destiny attempting to make your stronger. Just see it for what it is. A Life-Thing.

Then when it happens, do what you just to get your life back on track.

Don't make this process a big ordeal! Just do it. Take what comes. Do what your must. Make the decisions you must make, guided by the choices that are laid out in front of you. Forgive if you have to. Forget if you must. And, move on, the best you can. Because believe me, this is life, there will always be monkey wrenches thrown in your gears.

Inside the Corner

People forever make assumptions about other people's relationships.

How many times have you found yourself discussion someone else and their relationship with their husband, wife, boyfriend, girlfriend, child, brother, sister, friend, roommate, or whomever? You may be discussing their interactions, you may have even heard something or witnessed some activities, but in essence you have no true understanding of what is going on between those people because you are not them.

We each enter into and come at relationships with our set of predisposed biases, interpersonal understandings, and psychological manifestations. For each of us, we choose to interact with someone or not.

In terms of family, sometimes we are forced into interpersonal relationships. Relationships that we would have never personally chosen to have. But, due to blood, we are stuck. Stuck, at least until adulthood. But then, some people stay involved even when they understand that particularly relationship is not functioning at a high level or they want to move on. They stay involved because that person is, *"Family."*

Like the old saying goes, *"Blood is thicker than water."* People forgive family members much easier than they forgive others.

Love is also a reason people interact. Interact when it is probably in their best interest to move on. Yet, they stay.

Desire, addiction, wanting to help, are all also reasons that people enter into and stay in relationships. All of these things and more define the basis of interactive personal relationships.

Once two people have joined forced, others discuss them. They question the reasons they are together, the psychical and psychological factors behind their meeting, and their ongoing interactions.

You discuss them. But YOU don't know!

Think about this... You are with a person. You hear people discussing or questioning the realities of that relationship. How many of those times have people been completely off-base with their conclusions? How many times have you become angry because someone outside of the relationship has even attempted to understand it? And, how many times have you lied when you have told others about the inside, inter-workings of that particular relationship just to keep them from getting up in your business?

All this adds up to one thing. You can never know the true insides of any other person's relationship. Many people, the people actually involved in the relationship, do not even take the time to completely understand it. So, stop wasting your Life-Time, trying to define something you can and will never understand. Instead, focus on defining and understanding your own relationships.

Any Less Enlightened?

In my mid to late teens and early twenties I spent a lot of time with Swami Satchidananda and his organization the Integral Yoga Institute. I was his West Coast soundman, so I got to set up his audio and recorded all of the many lectures he gave.

For those of you from a different era, it may be a bit difficult to understand, but spirituality was ramped throughout the West at this time. And, Swami Satchidananda was one of the big wigs. In fact, he was the one chosen to open Woodstock.

Anyway… People had and have always held onto this ideology of how a guru is supposed to behave. It is thought that they are only supposed to sit around and meditate, perform holy ceremonies, bless people, give profound advice, and stuff like that. Swami Satchidananda did do that. But, he was also a licensed pilot and he drove around in a big-finned '57 Cadillac.

One time I was at his house in Montecito, California. He was discussing how the radio in his car had gone out. So, he took it to the shop. The shop manager wanted to add on an extra hundred dollars or something like that to take out the radio before they fixed it. *Gurudev,* (as we called him), concluded that he should just take out the radio himself and give it to them.

I'm not even going to go into what it must have looked liked for this East Indian Guru, with long hair and a long beard, dressed in orange robes, to have driven into the shop in a gigantic vintage Cadillac. But, anyway… He took the radio out and gave it to them to repair. When it was done, he put it back in his car.

The question is, because he did that – because he could do that, does that make him any less holy, any less enlightened? Though some my hold onto an idealized image of how a guru is supposes to behave, my belief is that this action did not diminish him in any way. In fact, it provided an ideal example of what enlightenment should look like. Someone who does what is needed in life to get things done…

This is life. Don't believe that enlightenment is only off in some far away distant place. It is right here. In this here and now, while you are doing what needs to be done.

Sometime You Just Have To Buy a New Pair of Shoes

Have you ever purchased a new pair of shoes and you really liked them? Then, all of a sudden, on the first day you wore them, they got totally messed up. That felt pretty bad didn't it?

I remember the first time this happened to me. I was in junior high and I had just gotten a new pair of green suede Converse – which were pretty expensive for the time. I had this one friend who was crazy. And, I mean crazy. He ended up killing his stepmother. But, that is a whole different story… Anyway, there was a lot of construction going on around the K. Town, (Koreatown), section of L.A back then. Which is where I was living.

It was a winter evening. It had gotten dark very early. My friend and I were walking past this construction site. It was totally muddy. He suggested we go and explore it. My first thought was, *"That place is really a mess."* But me, being who I am, (even way back then), I was All-In. I have always been All-In. We dove in and got totally muddy. My shoes got trashed. When I got home that evening, my mother freaked.

Much later, I was in my twenties. There was this pair of shoes that I really loved. They were the kind that the cops wore back in the sixties and seventies. They had a saw tooth rubber sole. I found them at Sears. You couldn't buy them anywhere else as they had fallen out of favor. No one else was wearing them anymore, but they perfectly suited the big bulky shoe-look that I desired. I was over in Tokyo and I had scuffed them up. I was pretty upset. So, I went to one of the shoeshine experts over by Shinjuku Station and had him do his magic.

But, nada, he couldn't get it done – couldn't get the scuff out. He apologized, (in Japanese, of course). But, it was really me who felt sorry, as I hated to have people polish my shoes.

My shoes, they were done. One of them had a big scuff-mark across the top of it. Couldn't wear them anymore... And, couldn't buy another pair in Tokyo.

A year or so later, when the Rockport walking shoes begin to be created... Again, a big bulky shoe, just my style – but now they were designed for walking miles-upon-miles like tennis shoes and still look good when you went to hit a high-end restaurant that require hard shoes for entrance. All good...

I was in Kuala Lumpur. I don't know how it happened, as I had been bouncing around Southeast Asia for the past month or two, but, in any case, my shoes got scuffed and looked really bad. I gave them over to my hotel executive floor concierge to get them polished. I had a date and my shoes had not returned so a couple of hours later I call about my shoes and another concierge brings them to my door. One had been polished the other one had not. The problem was; these shoes originally had a reddish tint to them. The original concierge polished one with a brown polish that left one shoe red and one shoe brown. The guy thought I might not like this so he stopped. I told the new concierge, *"Whatever, just make them match."* But, he couldn't, as he could not find the shoe polish the other guy had used. I was stuck. I had two different colored shoes, a dinner date in an hour, and a plane to catch for Bangkok in the morning.

A couple of years ago I used to love wearing the Nike hiking shoes. They were colorful and very comfortable. I was heading to Tokyo with a girl on her first trip there so I knew there would be a lot of subway taking and a lot of walking. Tokyo is a big place… So me, I picked up a new pair. I get there. I start wearing them and they destroyed my feat. Not with blisters but just full-on pain. I had never had pain like that in my feet. It became hard to even take a step. Thanks Nike! In L.A. I would have just gone a bought another pair of shoes but in Tokyo it is a bit hard for me to find shoes that are big enough and when I do they cost like three or four hundred dollars for a pair that I would pay fifty or seventy-five dollars for in the States.

A week or so ago I was dong this music video. I was wearing a new pair of black Sketchers I had picked up. I was shooting the video with a windup, vintage 35mm movie camera in order to get that slight fluctuation in speed that it would provide so I wouldn't have to do it in post. The problem was, the D.P. I hired didn't get the concept of working handheld with a 40mm lens at close range and setting focus with a tape measure, so I would get great depth of field. So much for a degree from the film school at U.S.C. In any case, I ended up shooting most of the footage myself.

While shooting it, I was kneeling down on one leg for a lot of the time. I wanted a low angle, shooting up, in order to give the primaries a very specific look. By the end of the shoot, I looked down and my right shoe, (the leg I was kneeling down on most of the time), had developed massive creases in the leather. The problem was, the left shoe had none. Call me OCD but when I got home I try to bend the left shoe to match the right shoe. No luck. They just looked like a completely different pair of shoes.

This is the reality of life, sometimes you just have to buy a pair of new shoes. Though they may not be exactly what you want, they are new, they are unscuffed, unpainful, uncreased, and they will

protect your feet while they take you where you need to go.
    This is the Zen of shoes.

When Opportunity Comes Knocking

When most of us think of opportunity, we think about very-obvious opportunities such as a way to make more money, being offered a new job, meeting a really pretty person, or being ushered onto a pathway to live our dreams. Though these things certainly are opportunities, the reality of most life opportunities is that they are much more subtle this.

True life opportunities come in very abstract manners and you have to be conscious to see them appear. In fact, most opportunities that will actually lead you to something bigger in your life appear in ways that you will never expect. For example, someone may have liked your actions in a particularly situation and asks about your reasoning, someone may ask you a question about another person or a current life event, from one person you may meet another person that has the potential to open new doors for you, or you may notice something on the internet or in the news and you decide to look into it further.

These previous interactions are just a couple of examples about how the one thing will lead to another and the door of opportunity will be opened for you. But, take a moment now and think about times in your life when some abstract thing happened, when somebody said something to you but you did not respond, when you were introduced to a person and you did not follow up on cultivating that relationship, when you should have done something that you didn't do and later you realized that if you had made the effort your life would have evolved completely differently. Think about and define these things because these are subtle elements of life that set your Life-Course and your next set of available opportunities into motion.

There is the old saying, *"You only get one shot."* Though this is not an absolute truth in life as with every moment you have a chance to develop something new, what it does ideally depict is that once a chance, once an opportunity has passed you by, that particular opportunity will never be there again.

Many people live their lives in a space of complete oblivion to how they are interacting with the world – most do not even care. But, if you want to truly move forward in life, in a conscious manner, if you truly want to do good things with your life, than you must become acutely aware of what it taking place around you and what opportunities, as subtle as they may be, are being presented to you.

When opportunity comes knocking, answer the door.

Texting on Two Wheels

Since the dawning of texting, a few years ago, I think we have all encountered the benefits and the determents. Like when you are driving and the car next to you is slowly crossing over into your lane. You honk and they get back into their own lane. Then, when you drive by, you can see that they are texting.

The same goes for stoplights. The light turns green and the car in front of you sits there and sits there. Finally, you honk – they go. When you drive by giving them a dirty look, you glance over and see that their face is once again looking downwards at their phone and their fingers are texting away.

This is dangerous and people have been injured and have died because of texting while driving. Not good! But, most of us do it –at least from time to time.

Here in California they have made it illegal to text and drive or even hold your phone to your ear and drive. It's a pretty expensive ticket. But, look around… Everybody's still doing it.

I spent the last few days up in Santa Cruz. While I was there I saw a first. A first, at least for me. I was driving down the street and there was this hippie girl riding her bike. She had both hands on her phone so she was riding hands-free. She was busy looking at her phone and texting.

The original reason I took notice was, like a car, she was not paying attention and she was veering into my lane. If it had been a car, I would have honked. But, as she didn't have her hands on her handlebars, I didn't want to honk. I didn't want her to freak her out, and make her crash. So, I let her veer on into my lane and just slowed down

A car behind me eventually didn't like what was going on. He (or she) honked. As suspected/expected the girl almost lost her balance. And, she almost dropped her phone. She grabbed the handlebars, held onto her phone, turned around and yelled, *"Fuck you!"*

In retrospect it is pretty funny. I mean, I know in Santa Cruz the lifestyle is a little bit different from most regions around California. But, texting on two wheels? I don't know... We all do what we do, dominated by what availably life has provided us with.

Look around, there is art and there are Life-Realizations everywhere...

A Choice Lasts Forever

Right here, right now there area million choices you could make. Most people don't realize this. Most people feel that they are stuck – locked into doing what they are doing. Most people follow a pattern. They live the same script over-and-over again. But, every one of us can make a choice.

Choices are everywhere. You can get up right now, go outside, stay inside, go and do something else. This, *"Something else,"* can be very spontaneous. It can mean going and taking a walk, going for a drive, calling somebody up, anything… But, there is one rule that applies to all choices we make. That rule is; a choice lasts forever.

Why does a choice last forever? Because whatever we choose to do sets our next set of available life circumstances into motion. Whatever we do, whatever choice we make, affects our lives. If we choose to do something with someone else, or to someone else, then karma is set in motion.

There is no choice that is free onto itself. There is no choice that does not come with a price to pay.

Some people set out to make positive choices in their life. Some people make choices that mess with other people's lives. Both of these are choices. But, the ultimate outcome is very obvious. If you make good choices, try to do good things; the chances that good things are going to come to you are substantially better. If, on the other hand, you do bad things and mess with other people's lives, than bad things are probably going to come to you from the choices you have made.

All of life is based upon choice.

What are you doing with your life right now? Do you have a job? If you do, how did you get that job? Probably, you needed to make some money to survive and pay your bills and pay your rent. Whatever the cause, you made a decision to go out there, apply for the job, and then you decided to make the choice to accept it, if and when it was offered. What course of events did that choice set in motion in your life? For each person it is different. Some love and some hate their jobs. Some see a job as a life-experience; others see it as a life-waste of time. But, it is what it is. You made a choice and now you are living it. Most people, never even try to reevaluate their choices. They lock themselves into them and they stay stuck.

Are you in a committed relationship? If you are that means that you chose to go out there and seek a companion. That also means that you chose to enter into that relationship. As most of us have found out, some relationships go very bad. But, it was our choice to enter into them in the first place. So, who is to blame? No one but ourselves. Other relationships, however, define our lives in a very positive manner. Again, all based upon choice.

From whatever you have previously chosen to do, bases upon whatever choices you have made in the past; here you are, this is your life. Your previous choices have defined where you find yourself now.

This is your life. You can choose to do anything based upon your life circumstance and the choices you have previously made that set your life-course in motion.

Choice is everywhere. Choice is everything. What do you choose to do now that you understand, *a choice lasts forever?*

In or Out

I was flipping channels the other evening and I came upon a movie, *The Outfit,* just beginning on TCM. This movie is from 1973 and stars Robert Duvall, Joe Don Baker, Robert Ryan, and my buddy Karen Black. The reason it caught my eye is that I remember seeing it in the theaters back when it was first released.

Back then; long before videotape, DVD, and streaming, you pretty much had to see all the new movies in theaters, and that was that. ...Because if you didn't see them in theaters, when they were first released, you would never get to see them at all unless they made their way to late night T.V. But then, they were cut and interrupted with tons of commercials and all the etcetera.

For each generation there are defining factors. For the newest of our generation, the isolation of this digital age has pressed down upon them. I mean, everybody stays at home! They rarely go to the movies, waiting for the movie to be on DVD, cable, streaming, or downloaded from an illegal download site. But, all of that does not equal OUT, it only equals IN. And IN there is no experience. OUT is where life is born.

When I look back, through the perspective of age, the first breeding of this IN generation happened back in the later 70s. I remember the first time I played the game, Pong. A friend of mine, Saturday Jim and I used to drive from L.A. up to Canada a lot. In fact, after a lot of slow trips up the coast, we got it down to a science; L.A. to Vancouver in seventeen hours. Anyway we were on the ferry that takes cars from the Vancouver area over to Vancouver Island. It's a couple hour ride.

On the ferry, there it was, Pong. Previous to this, games were all played in places like Pinball Arcades. Again, an interactive meeting place. But, soon after Pong appeared to the masses, it also became the first home game. Then came the various game consoles, and gaming was born.

How many people stay at home and spend hour-upon-hour playing video games? Even if they are interacting online, that is not true human interaction. They are alone and stuck in their head. What kind of life is that?

Watching this movie again on T.V., all these years later, made me realize that the entire reason I remember this film, (because it is not all-that great), was the experience of going out to see it in a theater. I remember I saw it when I was a teenager living in what is now the K. Town section of L.A. I saw it with my friend Steve at one of the local theaters, The Embassy on Western. In fact, I can think back to the first movie I ever saw at that theater. It was when I was a very young boy. I saw the first James Bond film there, *Dr. No* with my mother and my grandmother.

Think about it, how many films do you remember the whole experience of seeing them in theaters and how many films to your remember the whole film-going experience when you watched them at home on your T.V. or computer?

As a young boy I remember seeing *Modesty Blaze* with my parents at the theater in Westchester, *Doctor Zhivago* with my friends when I lived in Inglewood. I remember seeing so many films at the Wiltern theater on Wilshire. Everything from *The Wild Bunch,* to *Superfly,* onto *Five Fingers of Death, Master of the Flying Guillotine, Two Lane Blacktop, Che, Butch Cassidy and the Sundance Kid, 2001 A Space Odyssey, THX 1138,* and the list goes on and on. I remember going to see *Easy*

Rider with my mother in '69 at this theater on Hollywood Blvd, over by Vermont. I was so upset after seeing what happened in that film... Then, there was this junky theater on Hollywood by Western, they did the $2.00 on Tuesdays thing. My friends and I, (and just me by myself sometimes), saw tons of great B-Movies there. I saw all the Spaghetti Westerns at that theater; everything from, *My Name is Nobody, Fist Full of Dynamite,* onto *Django, The Gunfight,* and the list goes on and on. I image that is the same for you. You remember the OUT.

Sure-sure IN is fun to when you're with someone you dig and you're having a good time. But then, that experience is based upon the personal interaction, not on what you are seeing or doing.

Don't exist only on the IN. OUT is where life is born. Don't lose all the things you can gain, all the life experiences you can have, all the people you can meet by being OUT. Remember, typing on your computer and interacting with people on the internet is not true interaction.

OUT is the birthplace for living life.

You Verses Who

Whenever I teach a course on filmmaking I always begin by detailing the number one rule of filmmaking, *"Everybody lies."* From actors onto filmmakers, in the film industry everyone lies about everything; from their age, to who they know, to the budget of their project, to who is involved in the project, to the process they are using for the creation of the project, to what is coming next in their career, and on and on… But, the fact of the matter is, throughout all aspects of life, pretty much, everybody lies. People lie about who they are, what they are, where they are from, where they are going, what they thinking, what they are doing, etc. This is life and that is the truth, most everybody lies.

One may think on the spiritual path that this would all be different. But, coming from someone who has been walking the spiritual path for the better part of my life I can say with some authority that lies abound on it, as well. The thing is, there is no degree for being spiritual. There is no school you must graduate from where you receive a certificate of authenticity. People just become. In many ways that is a good thing because spiritually is based upon self-realization but this is also where it gets very messy.

There are a lot of people out there who claim spirituality, who claim to know; they claim to be teachers, mediums, psychics, priests, yogis, whatever… But when no one is looking they are a complete emotional and psychological wreck on the inside but they are too locked into their own egos to go and get the psychological guidance that they need. Though they may have spirituality in their heart, they have stepped up to pulpit in an attempt to fill a hole in their being. Why? They desire admiration.

The problem is, from actions based upon these principals, spiritually has become so convoluted and so many people have followed these false teachers, expecting to find inner truth and answer but since the source was so misguided this could never occur.

Desiring admirations is not spiritual. Do spiritual teachers who desire admiration tell their students that is the reason they are doing what they do? No, because then they would have no students. Yet, they are still out there deceiving people. They are lying.

On the more physical levels of reality, people lie all the time. They lie about who they are, what they are, how much money they have, what their desires for another person truly are, they even lie to themselves about why they are doing what they are doing.

In the realms of physical reality, lying is justifiable because we are all taught that we must go after a goal and gain it no matter what. But, no matter what, commonly injures a lot of people in the process.

So, I guess, not only in filmmaking but also in life in general, the number on rule is, *"Everybody lies."* For better or for worse that is it. That is what we have to deal with. We can try to be better ourselves and that is a good start. ...For all the world beings with us. And, we can also embrace the knowledge that we now know the number one rule. From all of this we can attempt to be forgiving when we encounter it. An absolute answer, no. An absolute solution, no.

Welcome to life where there is no absolute answers or solutions.

Sometime You Get Cut

I was setting up for a photo shoot. I went to move this prop that I have handled a hundred times. Ouch, it cut my finger. Why/how? I don't know, it just did. I was bleeding. This is life: sometimes, out of nowhere, you get cut.

I think we have all experienced situations like this. Cut, when you don't expect it and certainly don't want it. But, there it is, the blood starts to flow.

I think back to a number of times in my life when this has happened. I remember back to when I was a little kid, this cat looked oh so friendly. I go up and pet it. It sat there purring. I leave, and scratch, it didn't want me to leave. Bad intention? No. But, did it hurt? Yes.

Once when I was seventeen, I was helping do some garden rearranging at my guru's house. The guy who was helping me moved a rock, it shipped, fell on my finger. It didn't break my finger or anything like that, but it did cut me pretty good. There I was working in the dirt with a big open cut... Some people would have freaked out and quit. That's not my nature. I worked on. Cleaned it up later.

Once, while we were filming *Max Hell Frog Warrior* at night, on the location we titled, *The Bridge of Broken Dream,* my character was walking along and, as it was vey dark, I didn't notice that there was a hole in the bridge: BAM I stepped into it – that action totaled my shin. I was bleeding pretty good. Did I stop the shot? No way. I kept working through the night. Later we went to one of our actress's houses to do a few more scenes. She looked at my leg as I pulled my pants loose from the dried blood and she couldn't believe how bad it looked. I laughed it off. I still have that scar to this day.

It is not always physical; people also emotionally cut you out of nowhere. How many times have you been cut by someone you were friends with or cared about and out of nowhere; slice – they did you in? How many times have you extended a hand of friendship to someone only to find out that they used your kindness against you?

Maybe you have behaved like this? Maybe you have done it?

People cut other people for all kinds of reasons. They want to exhibit power, they want to show someone that they are better or more than them. They want to hurt them. They want to show them that they do not care. Or, maybe they are simply blind to the emotions of another individual. All are bad reasons. But, that does not stop this type of behavior from occurring.

Just like a physical cut, getting emotionally cut by someone you know, hurts. After all that time and energy you put into the relationship, and they did that!

Sometimes you find yourself mad at a person who cut you for along time after the incident. You find your mind wandering back to them, what they did, and how that made you feel. But, you got to know, that's just life – most people are in it for themselves.

You've got to clean your cuts or they will get infected. You got to free your mind of the emotional injuries inflicted by others or it will haunt you and define the rest of your life. You've got to move on and keep doing. Sure, you may hold a physical or emotional scare forever. But, you cannot let that scar define your life. You cannot let the incident or your reaction to the incident define who you are.

Let a cut hurt only as long as it hurts, then forget the pain.

...About the Author

Scott Shaw is a prolific author, actor, filmmaker, composer, and photographer. He is recognized as one of the preeminent Martial Arts Masters of the Western world and is at the forefront of integrating spirituality into the Martial Arts. During his youth he became deeply involved with Eastern Meditative Thought. This guided him to Asia where he has been initiated into Buddhist, Hindu, and Sufi sects. Today, Shaw frequently returns to Asia, documenting obscure aspects of Asian culture in words and on film. He is a frequently featured contributor to Martial and Meditative Art journals and is the author of numerous books on Zen Buddhism, Yoga, Meditation, Asian Studies, Ki Science, and the Martial Arts.

...Scott Shaw's Books-in-Print include:

About Peace: A 108 Ways to Be At Peace When Things Are Out of Control
Advanced Taekwondo
Arc Left from Istanbul
Bangkok and the Nights of Drunken Stupor
Bangkok: Beyond the Buddha
Bus Ride(s)
Cambodian Refugees in Long Beach, California: The Definitive Study
Chi Kung For Beginners
China Deep
Echoes from Hell
Essence: The Zen of Everything
e.q.
Hapkido: Articles on Self-Defense
Hapkido: Essays on Self-Defense
Hapkido: The Korean Art of Self-Defense
Hong Kong: Out of Focus
Independent Filmmaking: Secrets of the Craft
In the Foreboding Shadows of Holiness
Israel in the Oblique
Junk: The Backstreets of Bangkok
Last Will and Testament According to the Divine Rites of the Drug Cocaine

L.A.: Tales from the Suburban Side of Hell

Los Angeles Skidrow: 1983

Marguerite Duras and Charles Bukowski:
    The Yin and Yang of Modern Erotic Literature

Mastering Health: The A to Z of Chi Kung

Nirvana in a Nutshell

On the Hard Edge of Hollywood

Pagan, Burma: Shadows of the Stupa

Sake' in a Glass, Sushi with Your Fingers:
    Fifteen Minutes in Tokyo

Scream: Southeast Asia and the Dream

Samurai Zen

Sedona: Realm of the Vortex

Shama Baba

Shanghai Whispers Shanghai Screams

Shattered Thoughts

Singaore: Off Center

South Korea in a Blur

Suicide Slowly

Taekwondo Basics

Ten to Thirty

The Ki Process:
    Korean Secrets for Cultivating Dynamic Energy

The Little Book of Yoga Breathing

The Little Book of Zen Mediation

The Most Beautiful Woman in Shanghai

The Passionate Kiss of Illusion
The Screenplays
The Tao of Chi
The Tao of Self Defense
The Voodoo Buddha
The Warrior is Silent:
    Martial Arts and the Spiritual Path
The Zen of Modern Life and the Reality of Reality
TKO: Lost Nights in Tokyo
Wet Dreams and Placid Silence
Yoga: A Spiritual Guidebook
Yosemite: End of the Winter
Zen Buddhism: The Pathway to Nirvana
Zen Filmmaking
Zen in the Blink of an Eye
Zen O'clock: Time to Be
Zen: Tales from the Journey
Zero One

www.ingramcontent.com/pod-product-compliance
Lightning Source LLC
Chambersburg PA
CBHW061258110426
42742CB00012BA/1966